The Romanians in
America and Canada

ETHNIC STUDIES INFORMATION GUIDE SERIES

Series Editor: Curtis W. Stucki, Head, Catalog Division, University of Washington Libraries, Seattle

Also in this series:

BASQUES IN AMERICA—*Edited by William A. Douglass and Richard Etulain**

BIBLIOGRAFIA CHICANA—*Edited by Arnulfo D. Trejo*

DUTCH AMERICANS—*Edited by Linda Pegman Doezema*

GERMAN-AMERICAN HISTORY AND LIFE—*Edited by Michael Keresztesi and Gary Cocozzoli*

ITALIAN AMERICANS—*Edited by Francesco Cordasco*

JEWISH AMERICANA—*Edited by Michael Keresztesi and Bette Roth**

UKRAINIAN AMERICANS—*Edited by Vladimir Wertsman and Aleksander Sokolyszyn**

*in preparation

The above series is part of the
GALE INFORMATION GUIDE LIBRARY

The Library consists of a number of separate series of guides covering major areas in the social sciences, humanities, and current affairs.

General Editor: Paul Wasserman, Professor and former Dean, School of Library and Information Services, University of Maryland

Managing Editor: Denise Allard Adzigian, Gale Research Company

The Romanians in America and Canada

A GUIDE TO INFORMATION SOURCES

Volume 5 in the Ethnic Studies Information Guide Series

Vladimir Wertsman

Senior Librarian
Brooklyn Public Library
New York

Gale Research Company
Book Tower, Detroit, Michigan 48226

0731375

144801

Library of Congress Cataloging in Publication Data

Wertsman, Vladimir, 1929—
    The Romanians in America and Canada.

    (Ethnic studies information guide series ; v. 5) (Gale
information guide library)
    Includes indexes.
    1. Romanian Americans—Bibliography. 2. Romanians
in Canada—Bibliography. 3. Romanian Americans—Directory.
4. Romanians in Canada—Directories. I. Title.
Z1361.R65W47 [E184.R8]   016.3058'49'071   80-191
ISBN 0-8103-1417-7

Dedicated to All Men and Women Who Had or Have
a Share in Preserving the Romanian Heritage in
American and Canada for Future Generations

VITA

Vladimir F. Wertsman is by training both a lawyer and a multilingual librarian, with degrees from his native Romania (LL.M. Summa Cum Laude, University A.I. Cuza, Iassy) and from the United States (M.S.L.S., Columbia University). He is a senior librarian on the professional staff of the Brooklyn Public Library, a member of the Ethnic Material Information Exchange Task Force (American Library Association), and a member of the International Social Science Honor Society. For several years Wertsman has been involved in various projects--including surveys, lectures, and editorial work--devoted to ethnic Americans from Eastern Europe, with special interest in Romanian Americans.

Wertsman has written THE ROMANIANS IN AMERICA: 1748-1974; THE RUSSIANS IN AMERICA: 1727-1975; THE UKRAINIANS IN AMERICA: 1608-1975; THE ARMENIANS IN AMERICA: 1618-1976; and contributed more than thirty articles to law, library, and philatelic periodicals.

His biography has been included in CONTEMPORARY AUTHORS, WHO'S WHO IN THE EAST, and WHO'S WHO IN ROMANIAN AMERICA.

CONTENTS

Contents

Contents

Contents

ACKNOWLEDGMENTS

Once again I am glad to acknowledge numerous individuals who, although dispersed all over the United States and Canada, had two important elements in common: a profound interest in my project, coupled with a wonderful spirit of cooperation.

In this context, my very special thanks go first to Veturia Manuila, Board of Directors, Iuliu Maniu American Romanian Relief Foundation; Gabriela Barbu, reference librarian, Iuliu Maniu American Romanian Relief Foundation; Stefan G. Thedoru, Cultural Department, Iuliu Maniu American Romanian Relief Foundation; Right Rev. Bishop Valerian Trifa, head of the Romanian Orthodox Episcopate of America; Rev. George C. Muresan, editor of UNIREA, Association of Romanian Catholics of America; Theodore Andrica, editor of the AMERICAN ROMANIAN REVIEW; Jill A. Brown, bibliographer, Genealogical Society of the Jesus Christ of Latter-Day Saints; and Hana Cipris, coordinator, Hamilton Multicultural Centre, Canada, for their time, patience, specialized knowledge, advice, and materials brought to my attention.

I am also indebted to George Alexe, editor of CREDINTA, Romanian Orthodox Missionary Archdiocese in America; Lester Annenberg, head of Sports Library, Time, Inc. New York; Mr. Adrian Baranga, editor of ECOURI ROMANESTI, Canada; Mrs. Orit Barna, poet and freelance artist, New York; Dr. Karl Bonutti, director of the Ethnic Heritage Studies Center, Cleveland, Ohio; Edna Chang, supervising librarian, Brooklyn Public Library; Serge Corvington, librarian, History Division, New York Public Library; Lucia Herwig, Coordinator Information Services, Toronto Public Library, Canada; Mara Livezeanu, medical student, Tufts Medical School, Boston; Kathleen Miller, Cataloging Department, Cleveland State University; Rowena B. Tingley, North American Baptist Fellowship; and Jeffry L. Wonder, deputy director, American Legion, for various forms of assistance during the research period.

INTRODUCTION

"The Romanians in the United States constitute a picturesque, sturdy group of newly made Americans of whom altogether too little is known," observed Christine Avghi Galitzi--herself a Romanian American--while presenting her doctoral thesis at Columbia University in 1929.

Contrary to Christine A. Galitzi's hopes and expectations, the situation did not change too much in the ensuing five decades. The Romanian Americans and Canadians, like many other small ethnic groups, were either neglected or treated superficially by several ethnic writers. Suffice it to mention, for instance, that in Carl Wittke's WE WHO BUILT AMERICA (1939; reprinted 1967), as well as in Joseph Hutchmacher's A NATION OF NEWCOMERS (1967) or Alberta Eiseman's FROM MANY LANDS (1970), no reference is made to Romanians, even though other Eastern European immigrants are discussed. From Barbara Kay Greenleaf's AMERICA FEVER: THE STORY OF AMERICAN IMMIGRATION (1967) we find out that the Romanians arrived before World War I wearing "long sheepskin coats in every season," while BROOKLYN IS AMERICA (1967) Ralph Foster Weld recorded only that the Romanians settled in every neighborhood of Brooklyn.

Obviously, such treatment is not only unfair, but also very far from the historic realities, experiences, accomplishments, and contributions of Romanians on American and Canadian soil.

The truth is that Romanian Americans have a recorded presence of more than two hundred years in America, going back to the year 1748 when (Samuel) Damian, a Romanian Orthodox priest fron Transylvania, popularized his electrical experiments, and even managed to engage Benjamin Franklin in a scientific conversation. During the Civil War, two Romanians bravely fought for the Union's cause: George Pomutz (15th Iowa Regiment), later elevated to the rank of general, and Nicholas Dunca (9th Volunteers of New York), a captain who gave his life at Cross Keyes, Virginia. Romanian immigration to America and Canada strongly increased at the turn of the twentieth century. The majority of Romanian-American immigrants came from Transylvania and Bucovina (two regions under Austro-Hungarian rule at that time), while Romanian Canadian immigrants came mostly from Dobrogea (a Romanian region adjacent to the

Introduction

Black Sea). The immigrants were driven from their native places by precarious social and economic conditions, coupled with political and national persecutions in the first case. Immigration continued between the two world wars, but on a reduced scale. A new flow of immigrants (refugees and exiles) came to America and Canada at the conclusion of World War II and in the following decades.

Presently, the Romanian Americans form a community of about 225,000–235,000 people, spread all over the United States, but with heavier concentrations in the states of New York, New Jersey, Pennsylvania, Ohio, Illinois, Michigan, Indiana, and California. In Canada, there are about 25,000–30,000 Romanians, settled in the provinces of Manitoba, Saskatchewan, Ontario, Alberta, and Quebec. The Romanian Americans and Canadians are mostly of Eastern Orthodox faith. The rest consist of Catholics (Eastern Rite) and Baptists. Their native language—to the extent that it is still spoken—is Romanian, a Romance language. However, it has been anglicized through the absorption of English words. Unlike their ancestors, who were mostly peasants, laborers, and craftsmen, today more than 95 percent of the Romanian Americans are involved in factory work, as technicians, foremen, or engineers, or in sales, small enterprises, and managerial and professional activities. In Canada, a sizable number of Romanians are still involved in agriculture.

Despite their comparatively small number, the Romanian ethnics have made interesting and valuable contributions in various fields. Constantin Brancusi (sculpture), George Enesco (music), Stella Roman (opera), Nicholas Georgescu-Roegen (economics), Mircea Eliade (history of religion), Eli Cristo-Loveanu (painting), George de Bothezat (aeronautics), Alexandru Papana (aviation), Traian Leucutia (radiology), Emil Palade, (1974 Nobel Prize winner in medicine), Alexandru Seceni (architecture and icons), Vasile Posteuca (poetry), Peter Neagoe (fiction), Theodore Andrica (journalism), and Charles Stanceu (sports) are just some of those who have achieved national and international prominence.

Since their settlement, the Romanian Americans and Canadians founded more than 100 churches, over 300 organizations, associations, lodges, and so forth, as well as more than 120 periodical publications and newspapers of different orientations. During both world wars, more than 15,000 Romanians joined the U.S. and Canadian armed forces, several thousands distinguished themselves on the battlefields, and hundreds gave their lives for the cause they believed in and defended.

In the past, writers, researchers, and librarians were concerned more with Romania's history, people, and economic, social, political, and other related aspects rather than with the Romanian ethnic experience in America and Canada. It is true that Romanian American organizations put out some interesting and relevant materials—both in Romanian and English—but such materials had a very limited circulation, were spread in various local archives, and were rarely or only partly reflected in standard reference sources in English. In the

1940s the Cultural Association of Americans of Romanian Descent intended to publish an extensive bibliography, but, unfortunately, the project never came to fruition. Only in recent years has the revival of interest in Romanian ethnicity, generated by the search for ethnic roots movement, produced a few new books and other materials on Romanian Americans and Canadians. Yet, the most recent publications, like those from the past, whether in English, Romanian, or bilingual, were not comprehensive reference works.

In light of these circumstances, the present volume appears to be the first endeavor to assemble and present a comprehensive and annotated guide on the subject of Romanians in America and Canada, aimed at helping ethnic scholars, teachers, researchers, librarians, students, and other interested categories. It is to be hoped that this too will broaden the sphere of research and publications on the above subject, and add new quantitative and qualitative dimensions of such nature that Christine Avghi Galitzi's remark--mentioned at the very beginning of this essay--truly becomes outdated forever.

The present guide covers the collective experience of Romanians in America and Canada, as well as individual contributions made by Romanians in both countries. It consists of two parts--"Bibliographic Compendium" and "Directories Addendum" --with more than nine hundred annotated items, which were culled from both English and Romanian sources on a selective basis.

Part 1, the "Bibliographic Compendium," contains mostly English titles. Besides special titles directly covering various facets of Romanian American and Canadian experience, several standard reference works were included and examined critically--as to their usefulness and extent of coverage--since researchers usually turn to such works first. Also books were included and discussed on various themes written by Romanian Americans or Canadians to facilitate finding the individual contributions made in diverse fields of life. Otherwise, researchers who are not familiar with Romanian names or ethnic background of authors could easily overlook these contributions. Romanian titles are always accompanied by English translations. Annotations are descriptive, but also critical whenever necessary. The information for each bibliographic entry contains author (or editor, compiler, etc.), title, and facts of publication.

Part 2, the "Directories Addendum," is not just a compilation of listings. Entries have annotations substantially augmenting the first part of the guide and intimately connected with it through numerous cross-references.

Each entry of the guide has been assigned a code number. The code numbers use a letter which refers to each main section (e.g., A to "General Reference Works," B to "The Humanities." Within each section, items are numbered consecutively. Each section is accompanied by explanatory notes regarding the items, meanings of abbreviations, or other aspects. The three indexes--name, title, subject--all refer to code numbers.

Unlike other ethnic groups, the Romanians' name can be spelled in three ways:

Introduction

Roumanian, Rumanian or Romanian. While the first form comes from the French "Roumanie," and the second from the German "Rumaenien," the third one is based on historic events. The name Romania, meaning the land of Romans, was given by Roman colonists. They occupied the territory that is known today as Romania under the reign and leadership of Emperor Trajan in the years 101-6 A.D., keeping it thereafter for almost two centuries.

Even though according to WEBSTER'S NEW INTERNATIONAL DICTIONARY (3d ed.), all three forms of spelling are correct, we opted for the form Romania, which, besides connoting the historical background mentioned above, is the official name of this country, and the Romanians themselves--whether in the United States, Canada, or in their land of origin--prefer it over the other forms. However, when the other forms of spelling were parts of titles, they were left intact.

Vladimir Wertsman

Part 1

BIBLIOGRAPHIC COMPENDIUM

This compendium consists of about four hundred entries offering bibliographic information on books, pamphlets, and periodical materials of special significance. A traditional arrangement is used: "General Reference Works," "Humanities," "Social Sciences," "History," "Pure and Applied Sciences," with appropriate subdivisions. Annotations are descriptive and critical. Several cross-references connect the compendium with the "Directories Addendum."

A. GENERAL REFERENCE WORKS

BIBLIOGRAPHIES

Acquisition Sources—General

A-1   BOOKS IN PRINT, 1978-79. AUTHORS, 2 vols.; TITLES, 2 vols.
New York: R.R. Bowker Co., 1978.

These standard bibliographic sets--useful to public, academic,
and special libraries--list current titles in print on or by
Romanian Americans. However, several important titles--in
English, Romanian, and bilingual--put out by Romanian
American or Romanian Canadian publishing houses are not included. Bibliographic lists for these special titles should be
requested directly from Romanian publishing houses. See entries I-1 to I-7.

A-2   SUBJECT GUIDE TO BOOKS IN PRINT, 1978-79. 2 vols. New York:
R.R. Bowker Co., 1978.

Standard bibliographic set geared to the companion volumes
cited above (entry A-1). Presently, only five titles are
listed on the subject of Romanian Americans: WHO'S WHO
IN ROMANIAN AMERICA by Serban Andronescu; NO SOU-
VENIRS: JOURNAL, 1957-1969 by Mircea Eliade; A STUDY
OF ASSIMILATION AMONG THE ROUMANIANS IN THE
UNITED STATES by Christine Avghi Galitzi; AN AMERICAN
IN THE MAKING by M.E. Ravage; and THE ROMANIANS
IN AMERICA: 1748-1974, by Vladimir Wertsman. See entries
A-39, B-63, B-68, C-3, C-9.

Acquisition Sources—Special

A-3   BOOK REVIEW DIGEST. 73 vols. New York: H.W. Wilson Co.,
1905-- . Index.

A standard multivolume and very useful reference work incorporating several reviews of books on or by Romanian Americans. Does not reflect English, Romanian, or bilingual titles published by Romanian-American or Romanian-Canadian houses. For such titles, reviews can be found only in Romanian-American and Romanian-Canadian periodicals. See entries H-1 to H-27.

A-4   Mark, Linda, ed. REFERENCE SOURCES, 1977. Ann Arbor, Mich.: Pierian Press, 1977. 430 p. Index.

This comprehensive selection and acquisition tool covers several subjects, including ethnic Americans. Lists only one source on Romanian Americans (see entry C-3).

Research Guides

A-5   Toma, Radu, comp. ROMANII DIN AMERICA [The Romanians of America]. Bucharest: Asociatia Romania, 1978. 234 p.

An annotated bibliography of Romanian and Romanian-American periodical literature and some books covering the period 1900-1946. Relevant sections on Romanian immigration and settlement in America, organizations, press, church, youth, assimilation, and letters, but very little on Romanian contributions to America. Special attention and space is devoted to ties between Romanian Americans and their land of origin. Contains 970 entries, but no index.

A-6   U.S. Library of Congress. Slavic and Central European Division. Compiled by Stephen Fischer-Galati. RUMANIA: A BIBLIOGRAPHIC GUIDE. Washington, D.C.: Government Printing Office, 1963. 75 p. Pap.

A brief descriptive bibliographic survey arranged by subject and covering all areas of knowledge except medicine and natural sciences. Includes monographs and periodicals, mostly in Romanian. Useful to researchers interested in general background information on the country of origin and the heritage of Romanian immigrants to America and Canada. Contains 648 annotated items.

Periodical Literature

A-7   "Biblioteca din Cleveland si Cartile Romanesti" [The Cleveland Library and the Romanian books]. AMERICA, July 16, 1930, pp. 1-2.

Examination of the Romanian book holdings at the Cleveland Public Library, at that time serving the most numerous Romanian-American community.

A-8   "Catalogul Cartilor Romanesti Importate ale Librariei Biblioteca Romano-
       Americana din Youngstown" [The catalog of Romanian imported books
       at the Romanian American bookstore and library of Youngstown, Ohio].
       AMERICA, January 31, 1930, pp. 3-5.

       Listings of Romanian books (on various subjects) imported from
       Romania and of interest to first-generation Romanian Americans
       at that time.

A-9   Gratiaa, Josephine. "Romanians in the United States and Their Rela-
       tions to Public Libraries." LIBRARY JOURNAL, May 1, 1922, pp. 400-
       404.

       A study incorporating a list of Romanian American newspapers,
       Romanian American communities, and the number of Romanian
       books kept at the local libraries, as well as titles in which
       the patrons were interested. Preceded by a short section on
       the historical and social background of Romanian immigrants
       to America. This is the first material written by a Romanian
       American librarian.

CATALOGS

A-10   Bogart, Gary L., and Fidell, Estelle, eds. PUBLIC LIBRARY CATALOG.
       6th ed. New York: H.W. Wilson Co., 1974. 1,543 p. Index.

       This standard classified and annotated list of nonfiction books
       recommended for public and college libraries does not have
       any entries on Romanian Americans. However, its 1976 supple-
       ment lists THE ROMANIANS IN AMERICA: 1748-1974 by
       Vladimir Wertsman (see entry C-3).

A-11   Kimball, Stanley B., ed. SLAVIC-AMERICAN IMPRINTS: A CLASSI-
       FIED CATALOG OF THE COLLECTION OF LOVEJOY LIBRARY.
       Edwardsville: Southern Illinois University, Libraries, 1972. viii, 242 p.

       Although Romanian is a Romance and not a Slavic language,
       this catalog includes--along with other non-Slavic items--eight
       Romanian American publications published between 1911 and
       1922 which deal with physical education, religion, English
       grammar and letter writing, and Romanian immigration to
       America. All are in Romanian. Interesting for research pur-
       poses.

A-12   West, Dorothy Herbert, and Fidell, Estelle A., eds. STANDARD CATA-
       LOG FOR PUBLIC LIBRARIES. 4th ed. New York: H.W. Wilson Co.,
       1959. 1,349 p. Index.

       Standard reference work of nonfiction books destined for pub-
       lic and college libraries. Recommends only one item on the

subject of Romanian Americans: a section from ONE AMERICA
by Francis J. Brown and Joseph S. Roucek (see entry C-5).

LIBRARY RESOURCES

Research Guides

A-13   Ash, Lee, comp. SUBJECT COLLECTIONS. 4th ed. New York: R.R.
Bowker Co., 1974. 908 p.

> A guide to special book collections and subjects kept in uni-
> versity, public, and special libraries. For Romania and Ro-
> manians it makes references to University of California, Los
> Angeles, Kent State University, Pittsburgh University, Univer-
> sity of Illinois, and the New York Public Library. Emphasis
> is on the history, language, culture, and civilization of the
> country of origin rather than on Romanian immigration and
> contributions to America and Canada.

A-14   Williams, Sam P., comp. GUIDE TO THE RESEARCH COLLECTIONS
OF THE NEW YORK PUBLIC LIBRARY. Chicago: American Library
Association, 1975. 335 p. Index.

> Useful reference tool. Describes in detail library holdings on
> Romania and Romanians, including immigration to America and
> Canada. The New York Public Library has a sizable collec-
> tion on Romanian Americans as well as some Romanian Ameri-
> can publications.

A-15   Wynar, Lubomy R., and Buttlar, Lois, eds. GUIDE TO ETHNIC MU-
SEUMS, LIBRARIES AND ARCHIVES IN THE UNITED STATES. Kent,
Ohio: Program for the Study of Ethnic Publications, School of Library
Science, Kent State University, 1978. 390 p. Index.

> Comprehensive directory to noted resource centers of seventy
> ethnic groups, including the Romanian Americans. Describes
> collections, availability to public, publications, programs,
> and services provided by the ethnic institutions.

A-16   "Cleveland Romanian Cultural and Art Center." AMERICAN ROMANIAN
REVIEW 1 (July 1977): 5-12.

> A very good description of the most important Romanian American
> and Canadian ethnographic museum and library, with more than
> 2,500 books. Accompanied by relevant illustrations.

A-17   Dwyer, Joseph D., comp. THE ROMANIAN AMERICAN COLLECTION.
Ethnic Collection Series, no. 7. St. Paul: University of Minnesota,
Immigration History Research Center, 1976. 6 p. Pap.

A pamphlet describing the holdings on Romanians in America at the Immigration Research Center: 150 books, 22 serial titles, 9 current newspapers, and 9 manuscript collections donated by the Iuliu Maniu Relief Foundation, the Romanian Orthodox Episcopate in America, and the Union and League of Romanian Societies in America.

A-18 THE ROMANIAN AMERICAN HERITAGE CENTER. Jackson, Mich.: Romanian Orthodox Episcopate of America, 1975. 32 p. Pap.

A pamphlet with documents (resolutions, minutes, governing by-laws) regarding the establishment of the Romanian American Heritage Center dedicated to the study, research, and preservation of materials on the Romanian ethnic group in America and Canada. The center is open to individuals as well as to Romanian American and Canadian religious and fraternal organizations.

SOCIETIES

General Guides

A-19 ENCYCLOPEDIA OF ASSOCIATIONS. 13th ed. 3 vols. Edited by Nancy Yakes and Denise Akey. Detroit: Gale Research Co., 1979. Annual. Index.

Standard comprehensive reference work providing good coverage for all ethnic groups. It lists six Romanian American national organizations with their addresses, membership, purpose, publications, annual meetings. Also, lists three inactive organizations. Good for quick reference.

A-20 Wynar, Lubomyr R., ed. ENCYCLOPEDIC DIRECTORY OF ETHNIC ORGANIZATIONS IN THE UNITED STATES. Assisted by Lois Buttlar and Anna T. Wynar. Littleton, Colo.: Libraries Unlimited, 1975. xxiii, 441 p. Index.

Similar information as in the previous entry, but lists a few local organizations in addition to national organizations. Also mentions their publications. Good for quick reference.

Regional Guides

A-21 Anderson, James M., ed. ETHNIC DIRECTORY II- ETHNI-CITY: A GUIDE TO ETHNIC DETROIT. Detroit: Michigan Ethnic Heritage Studies Center, 1976. 144 p. Pap.

Short description of the Romanian ethnic group in Detroit, and listings of churches, organizations, shrines, picnic grounds, radio stations, publications, and businesses. Statistical appendix.

A-22   Sun Newspapers and Nationalities Service Center.   GREATER CLEVE-
       LAND NATIONALITIES DIRECTORY.   Cleveland: Sun Newspapers,
       1974.   162 p.   Pap.

       Lists Romanian organizations of Cleveland--fraternal, cultural,
       religious, youth, ladies auxiliaries.

Periodical Literature

A-23   "National Organization."   NEW PIONEER 3 (July 1945):   29-45.

       A complete list of Romanian American and Canadian national
       and local organizations, publications, churches, and radio
       stations at the conclusion of World War II.   Arranged alpha-
       betically by locality.   Useful for historical research.

NOTE: For a complete list of Romanian American and Canadian national and
local organizations and institutions, both active and retrospective, see entries
F-1 to F-148.

ENCYCLOPEDIAS

A-24   Pearson, Kenneth, ed.   ENCYCLOPEDIA CANADIANA.   10 vols.
       Ottawa: Grolier of Canada, 1977.   Index.

       In this prestigious set, there is an entry "Romanian Origin,
       People of" by George Nan, a Romanian Canadian Orthodox
       priest (vol. 9, pp. 91-92).   The article describes, among
       other topics, Romanian immigration and settlement in Canada,
       religion, churches, social life, societies, and press.

A-25   Thernstrom, Stephan, ed.   HARVARD ENCYCLOPEDIA OF AMERICAN
       ETHNIC GROUPS.   Cambridge, Mass.: Harvard University Press, in
       press.   1,200 p.   Index.

       Comprehensive, scholarly work covering more than one hundred
       American groups, including the Romanians.   Sheds light on
       original land, people, and culture, Romanian immigration and
       settlement in America, economic life, education, social life,
       organization, politics, religion, family life, cultural heritage,
       and relations with country of origin.   The entry on Romanian
       Americans includes a bibliography and map.

A-26   Wasserman, Paul, and Morgan, Jean, eds.   ETHNIC INFORMATION
       SOURCES OF THE UNITED STATES: A GUIDE TO ORGANIZATIONS,
       AGENCIES, FOUNDATIONS, INSTITUTIONS, MEDIA, COMMERCIAL
       AND TRADE BODIES, GOVERNMENT PROGRAMS, RESEARCH INSTI-
       TUTES, LIBRARIES AND MUSEUMS, RELIGIOUS ORGANIZATIONS,
       BANKING FIRMS, FESTIVALS AND FAIRS, TRAVEL AND TOURIST
       OFFICES, AIRLINE AND SHIP LINES, BOOKDEALERS AND PUBLISHERS'

REPRESENTATIVES, AND BOOKS, PAMPHLETS AND AUDIOVISUALS ON SPECIFIC ETHNIC GROUPS. Detroit: Gale Research Co., 1976. xv, 758 p. Index.

> Extensive coverage of most ethnic groups. The section devoted to Romanian Americans (pp. 529-33) includes fraternal and religious organizations, newspapers, radio programs, books and pamphlets, as well as audiovisual materials. However, the films are mostly on Romania rather than Romanians in America.

PERIODICALS

Reference Guides

A-27　American Council for Nationalities Service. THE ETHNIC PRESS IN THE UNITED STATES. New York: American Council for Nationalities, 1974. Unpaged. Pap.

> A compilation covering several ethnic groups, including the Romanian Americans. Lists only five periodicals: AMERICA, UNIREA, SOLIA, ROMANIA and ROMANIAN BULLETIN, with addresses and names of editors. Incomplete and outdated.

A-28　1979 EDITOR AND PUBLISHER INTERNATIONAL YEARBOOK. New York: Editor and Publisher, 1979. Unpaged.

> Basic reference tool for the newspaper industry in America and Canada. Although it claims to be of encyclopedic nature, lists two Romanian American periodicals in the foreign-language publications section: SOLIA and AMERICA: AMERICAN RO- MANIAN NEWS.

A-29　'79 AYER DIRECTORY OF PUBLICATIONS. 111th ed. Philadelphia: Ayer Press, 1979. 1,246 p. Index.

> Despite the reputation and usefulness of this standard reference work, its foreign-language publications section is very weak for Romanian periodicals. Lists only SOLIA, a religious news- paper, and AMERICAN ROMANIAN NEWS, which ceased pub- lication. Shows addresses, circulation, price, and frequency.

A-30　THE STANDARD PERIODICAL DIRECTORY. 6th ed. New York: Ox- bridge Communications, 1978. 1,680 p. Index.

> Standard and well-known reference tool, claiming to be the largest (60,000 entries) and most authoritative guide to U.S. and Canadian periodicals. However, mentions only four Roma- nian American periodicals: AMERICA, LUMINATORUL, SOLIA, UNIREA, with the largest circulation. Shows circulation, price, frequency. Good for quick reference.

A-31   ULRICH'S INTERNATIONAL PERIODICAL DIRECTORY, 1977-78. New
        York: R.R. Bowker Co., 1978. 2,096 p. Index.

>   Standard classified guide to current American and foreign peri-
>   odicals, arranged by various subjects. Lists only two Romanian
>   American periodicals--AMERICA and SOLIA--with very sketchy
>   annotations.

A-32   Wynar, Lubomyr R., ed. ENCYCLOPEDIC DIRECTORY OF ETHNIC
        NEWSPAPERS AND PERIODICALS. Littleton, Colo.: Libraries Unlimited,
        1972. 260 p. Index.

>   Comprehensive reference work covering fifty-three ethnic groups,
>   including Romanian Americans. Lists seven periodicals:
>   AMERICA, AMERICAN-ROMANIAN NEWS, LUMINATORUL,
>   ROMANIA, SOLIA, UNIREA, and ROMANIAN BULLETIN.
>   Annotations reflect address, editor, circulation, frequency,
>   price. Superseded by entry A-33.

A-33   Wynar, Lubomyr R., and Wynar, Anna T., eds. ENCYCLOPEDIC DIRECTORY
        OF ETHNIC NEWSPAPERS AND PERIODICALS IN THE UNITED STATES.
        2d ed. Littleton, Colo.: Libraries Unlimited, 1976. 248 p. Index.

>   This revised edition brought a change in the "Romanian Press"
>   section. AMERICAN-ROMANIAN NEWS was eliminated (ceased
>   publication) and replaced with CREDINTA. The rest of the
>   items remained the same. Also, there are references to the Ro-
>   manian American press in the editor's introduction and in statis-
>   tical appendixes. Good for quick reference, but incomplete.

NOTE: For a complete list of Romanian American and Canadian periodicals,
both active and retrospective, see entries H-1 to H-122.

Monograph—General

A-34   Park, Robert. THE IMMIGRANT PRESS AND ITS CONTROL. New
        York: Harper and Brothers, 1922. 488 p.

>   In this extensive study, dealing with about one thousand publi-
>   cations put out by forty-three American immigrant groups at the
>   beginning of the 1920s, the Romanian press is discussed, but on
>   a reduced scale compared to other ethnic groups. Good for
>   historical research.

Monograph—Special

A-35   Trifa, Bishop Valerian. SOLIA: ISTORIA VIETII UNEI GAZETTE RO-
        MANESTI IN AMERICA [Solia: The history of a Romanian American
        newspaper]. Jackson, Mich.: Romanian Orthodox Episcopate of America,
        1961. 80 p. Pap.

>   A commemorative issue devoted to SOLIA [The Herald], the

official organ of the Romanian Orthodox Episcopate of America, in its twenty-fifth year of existence. Well documented and appended by a list of Romanian retrospective and active periodicals. Also, a biographical sketch of Ion G. Gaspar, a noted Romanian American printer.

SOURCES ON JOURNALISM

Monographs

A-36 Adamic, Louis. MY AMERICA. New York: Harper and Brothers, 1938. xiii, 669 p. Index.

> In this book, devoted to various contributions made by ethnic Americans, there is a section on Theodore Andrica. It is the story of a Romanian immigrant who became a noted journalist in Cleveland and later editor of the Nationalities Press of the same city. See also entries C-28, C-32 to C-34.

A-37 Valahu, Mugur. KATANGA CIRCUS: A DETAILED ACCOUNT OF THREE U.N. WARS. New York: Robert Speller & Sons, 1964. 364 p.

> A Romanian American journalist's description of the secessionist war in Katanga, Congo, during the years 1960-62. Considered the most complete and impartial narrative on Katanga events. But the construction of phrases in English leaves much to be desired in several cases.

Periodical Literature

A-38 "John Florea." LIFE, November 5, 1945, p. 108.

> Biography and picture of John Florea, a noted Romanian American photographer and correspondent for LIFE magazine during World War II. He covered Europe and the Pacific, including the Japanese surrender aboard the U.S.S. MISSOURI. See also entries B-157, B-158.

BIOGRAPHY

A-39 American Institute for Writing Research, ed. WHO'S WHO IN ROMANIAN AMERICA. Compiled by Serban Andronescu. New York: Andronescu-Windhill, 1976. 190 p. Pap.

> A compilation encompassing short biographies of some five hundred Americans who were born in Romania or are interested in Romanian studies, regardless of their ethnic or religious

background, social status, or political affiliations. Also, appendix of religious organizations, churches, press, radio programs. Based on questionnaires sent by the compiler. No index, just a table of contents.

SOURCES ON GENEALOGY

Ethnic Origins

PERIODICAL LITERATURE

A-40   Botez, Ion. "A Short Survey of the Neolatins of the Near East." AMERICA, May 31-June 1, 1914, p. 1.

   The first English article in the Romanian American press dealing with the Latin background of the Romanians, their culture and civilization. Interesting material for historical research.

A-41   Popa-Deleu, John. "The Romanians Are Not Slavs." NEW PIONEER 1 (July-September 1943): 28-29.

   Short but well-documented article demonstrating the intimate relationship between the Romanian and Latin languages, with concrete examples. Aimed at refuting theories according to which the Romanians were confused with Slavs.

Names

PERIODICAL LITERATURE

A-42   Motzu, Joan. "A Genealogical Survey of Romanian Names." NEW PIONEER 2 (July 1944): 17-18; (October 1944): 46-48; 3 (January 1945): 37-38; (April 1945): 22-23; (October 1945): 30-32; 4 (January 1946): 38-39; (July 1946): 21-22.

   An extensive study tracing Romanian names, their meanings, roots and regions of origin. Many of the names discussed in the article can be found among the Romanians who settled in America and Canada. Of special research value.

Flags

PAMPHLET

A-43   Theodoru, S.G. A WALLACHIAN FLAG. New York: Author's Publications, 1977. 18 p. Pap.

   Detailed description of an old flag of Wallachia, (Romanian

region) discovered by the author in an Austrian museum. Preceded by a general introduction on Romanian flags. Illustrations. The author is a Romanian American poet. See also entry B-83.

DISSERTATIONS

A-44 DISSERTATION ABSTRACTS: ABSTRACTS OF DISSERTATIONS AND MONOGRAPHS IN MICROFILM. 26 vols. Ann Arbor, Mich.: Xerox University Microfilms, 1952-- . Monthly. Index.

Standard compilation of doctoral dissertations in various fields. Lists about two dozen titles on Romanian subjects between 1929 and 1977, but the great majority of them deal with Romanian language or civilization topics which are not related to Romanian Americans or Canadians. Relevant dissertations were included in different sections of this guide. See entries B-119, C-21, E-14, E-15.

B. THE HUMANITIES

PHILOSOPHY

Monographs

B-1   Cioran, E[mil]. M. THE FALL INTO TIME. Tr. from French by Richard
        Howard. Intr. by Charles Newman. New York: Quadrangle Books,
        1971. 183 p.

        A philosophical work reflecting the author's conception that the
        course of history did not produce the slightest improvement in
        man's lot. Emil Cioran is a Romanian exile, presently
        living in France, but with considerable appeal to Romanian
        intellectual circles from America, Canada, and other countries.

B-2   _____. A SHORT HISTORY OF DECAY. Tr. from French by Richard
        Howard. New York: Viking Press, 1976. 181 p.

        A collection of aphoristic page-long essays examining the
        philosophical virtues of the twentieth century: man and history,
        human progress, religion, fanaticism, love, modern sciences,
        philosophy.

RELIGION—GENERAL

Reference—Guides and Handbooks

B-3   Foy, Felician A., ed. 1979 CATHOLIC ALMANAC. Huntington, Ind:
        Our Sunday Visitor, 1979. 703 p. Index.

        Valuable encyclopedic volume of Catholic information, statis-
        tics, directories. In the section "Eastern Rites in the United
        States," there is an entry on Romanian Catholics and their
        organization (p. 319).

B-4   Jaquet, Constant H., ed. YEARBOOK OF AMERICAN AND CANADIAN
        CHURCHES: 1978. Nashville, Tenn.: Abingdon Press, 1978. 271 p.
        Index.

This standard reference book includes a short history of the Romanian Orthodox Church in America and Canada, its organizational structure, and addresses and officers of two existing religious bodies: the Romanian Orthodox Espiscopate of America and the Romanian Orthodox Missionary Archdiocese of America (pp. 86 and 127). No information on Romanian Baptists and Catholics.

B-5   Mead, Frank S., ed. HANDBOOK OF DENOMINATIONS IN THE UNITED STATES. 6th ed. Nashville, Tenn.: New York: Abingdon Press, 1975. 320 p. Index.

This familiar handbook contains a short presentation of the Romanian Orthodox Episcopate of America and its organizational structure. Also mentions the Romanian Catholics in the chapter devoted to Eastern Rite groups. Good for quick reference purposes, but incomplete. Romanian Baptists and the Romanian Orthodox Missionary Archdiocese in America are totally omitted.

Romanian Baptist Churches

PERIODICAL LITERATURE AND PAMPHLETS

B-6   Crisan, George. "Romanian Baptists in America." CALENDARUL ZIARULUI AMERICA (1976): 191-93.

Background information on Romanian Baptists, their history, aims, achievements, and attitude towards land of origin.

B-7   "Prima Biserica Romana Baptista din Cleveland, Ohio" [The First Romanian Baptist Church of Cleveland, Ohio]. LUMINATORUL (September 1929), p. 6.

Short article regarding the establishment of the church and its development before and after World War I.

B-8   Trutza, Peter, and Jones, V.W. THE HISTORY OF THE ROMANIAN BAPTISTS IN AMERICA. Cleveland: Romanian Baptist Association of U.S.A. and Canada, 1953. 72 p. Pap.

Pamphlet devoted to the immigration of Romanian Baptists to America, their settlement and establishment of churches, organizations, press, and social life.

Romanian Catholic Churches

PERIODICAL LITERATURE

B-9   Association of Romanian Catholics of America. THE UNIREA ALMANAC.

East Chicago, Ind.: Romanian Catholic Publishing Co., 1976.
176 p.

> Bicentennial and bilingual issue. Besides directories of par-
> ishes and priests, and a religious calendar, there are interest-
> ing articles on the preservation of the Romanian Catholic
> Church in America, the use of the Romanian language in
> church services, and Romanian Catholic organizations (ARCA
> and ARCAYD) and their significance. Relevant illustrations.

B-10   Gruitza, Sue. "St. John's Parish in Sharon: A Typical Romanian-
American Parish." UNIREA ALMANAC (1977): 63-71.

> This article is devoted to a Romanian Catholic church estab-
> lished in 1908 by Father Alexandru Nicolescu in Sharon,
> Pennsylvania. Outlines its development, priests who served
> it, and outstanding parishoners. Picture of the church.

B-11   Muresan, Rev. Fr. George. "ARCAYD, Organization for Romanian
Catholic Youth." ROMANIAN SOURCES 1 (1975): 39-40.

> A short article dealing with the organization created by the
> Association of Romanian Catholics of America in 1972 to in-
> volve youth in parish life and activities.

B-12   "What is ARCA?" ROMANIAN CATHOLIC CHURCH ALMANAC
(1972): 115-19.

> A presentation of the Association of Romanian Catholics of
> America (ARCA)--its purpose, function, membership, govern-
> ing structure, policy-making, meetings, and conventions.
> Includes the 1971 text of the ARCA constitution, revised from
> the original 1948 text.

Romanian Orthodox Episcopates of America

COMMEMORATIVE ISSUES

B-13   The Romanian Orthodox Episcopate of America. ALBUM ANIVERSAR
[Anniversary album]. Detroit: Admiral Printing Co., 1954. 184 p.

> Devoted to the twenty-fifth anniversary of the Romanian
> Orthodox Episcopate of America, this book sheds light on
> Romanian immigration to America, history of the Romanian
> Orthodox Church, establishment of the episcopate in 1929,
> its subsequent development, and various parishes. Sup-
> plemented by numerous illustrations and relevant documents.

B-14   _____. CALENDARUL SOLIA (1976). Jackson, Mich.: 1976. 284 p.

Bicentennial issue. Except for the religious calendar, the
entire issue is in English. It contains a directory of parishes
in America and Canada, the historical background of the
episcopate, and short biographies of past and present priests.
Numerous illustrations of church buildings, parish, youth, and
ladies auxiliaries activities.

B-15 _____. TWENTY YEARS OF PICTORIAL REVIEW: 1952-1972. Grass
Lake, Mich.: 1972. 124 p.

A collection of pictures highlighting important phases of the
episcopate's activities during two decades. Focuses on members of the clergy, church buildings in America and Canada,
youth and ladies auxiliaries work. Excellent pictures. Short
text deals with the episcopate's history, major events, clergy,
auxiliaries, education camps, external relations, and bishop's
visits.

SPECIAL ISSUE—YOUTH

B-16 Lascu, Traian. THE AMERICAN ORTHODOX YOUTH: A SHORT
HISTORY. Grass Lake, Mich.: Romanian Orthodox Episcopate, 1974.
145 p. Pap.

A detailed account of the history and development of the
American Romanian Orthodox Youth, its objectives and accomplishments in various fields: conventions, church projects,
summer camps, athletics, educational activities. Accompanied
by very good illustrations. The author was a noted leader of
the organization.

PERIODICAL LITERATURE AND PAMPHLETS

B-17 GETTING ACQUAINTED WITH THE ROMANIAN ORTHODOX EPISCO-
PATE OF AMERICA. Jackson, Mich.: Romanian Orthodox Episcopate
of America, 1977. 20 p. Pap.

A small but useful pamphlet directory containing the origin
of the Romanian Orthodox Church, its evolution in America
under two bishops (Morusca and Trifa), headquarters, publications, organizations, canonical jurisdiction, and parishes.

B-18 Hategan, Rev. Fr. Vasile. FIFTY YEARS OF THE ROMANIAN ORTHO-
DOX CHURCH IN AMERICA. Jackson, Mich.: Romanian Orthodox
Episcopate of America, 1959. 40 p. Pap.

Pamphlet dealing with the beginnings of Romanian immigration
and settlement in America and Canada, the development of
parishes, their organization, problems, consolidation, and new

directions under the leadership of the Romanian Orthodox Episcopate of America. Includes a list of main chronological events and a list of parishes.

B-19   "Pioneer Romanian Priests in U.S." AMERICAN ROMANIAN REVIEW 1 (September 1977): 9-16.

An article devoted to Epaminonda Lucaciu (Romanian Catholic) and Moise Balea (Romanian Orthodox), two pioneer priests who played an important role in the development of the denomination's first parishes. Accompanied by pictures.

B-20   "The Search for a Bishop." CALENDARUL SOLIA (1977): 90-156.

An extensive article devoted to the historical background of the Romanian Orthodox Church in America, causes leading to the establishment of the Romanian Orthodox Episcopate in America under the leadership of Bishop Valerian D. Trifa in 1952, and its separation from the Romanian Patriarchate with headquarters in Bucharest, Romania. Supplemented by several relevant documents, letters, court proceedings and decisions.

B-21   Trifa, Bishop Valerian D., and Hategan, Rev. Fr. Vasile. THE ORTHODOX CHURCH TODAY AND THE ROMANIAN CHURCH TODAY. Cleveland: Romanian Orthodox Episcopate of America, 1964. 48 p. Pap.

The first part of this pamphlet, written by Trifa, deals with the history of the Orthodox Church, its dogma, difference from the Catholic Church, existing patriarchates, and the situation of the Romanian Orthodox Church both in Romania and America. The second part sheds light on Romanian church history. Includes questions and topics for student discussions.

The Romanian Orthodox Missionary Archdiocese in America

MONOGRAPH

B-22   Bratu, Petre. REFORMATORUL ROMANO-AMERICAN [The Romanian American reformer]. Cleveland: Uniunea Societatilor Romane, 1911. 150 p.

A study suggesting the necessity of changes in Romanian American church practices and dogmas, flexibility, and adaptability to the new environment. Expresses a Romanian American layman's view.

PERIODICAL LITERATURE AND PAMPHLETS

B-23   Panciuk, Rev. Fr. Mircea. "The Romanian Orthodox Church of Hairy Hill, Alberta" and "The Holy Ghost Romanian Orthodox Church of Hamlin, Alberta." CALENDARUL CREDINTA (1974): 105-9.

Short history and pictures of two Romanian Canadian churches, both established at the beginning of the twentieth century.

B-24   The Romanian Orthodox Missionary Episcopate in America. THE ROMANIAN ORTHODOX MISSIONARY EPISCOPATE IN AMERICA: A SHORT HISTORY. Detroit: 1967. 15 p. Pap.

A pamphlet containing three short articles on the nature of the religious body, its evolution and jurisdiction. Subordinated to the Romanian Orthodox Patriarchate with headquarters in Bucharest, Romania.

B-25   Ursul, George R. "The Old Church in the New World." CALENDARUL CREDINTA (1967): 110-15.

Short presentation of the first Romanian Orthodox churches in America and Canada, their ties with the land of origin. The author is a Romanian American who teaches at Emerson College in Boston.

SPECIAL ISSUES

B-26   The Romanian Orthodox Missionary Archdiocese in America. CALENDARUL CREDINTA (1976). Detroit: 1976. 260 p.

Bicentennial issue containing the Declaration of Independence, the Bill of Rights, the American Creed, and an article dealing with the relationship between the Romanian Americans and the bicentennial. Also included are a religious calendar, a directory of parishes and priests in America and Canada, numerous illustrations with church buildings, parishioners, family events.

Religious Myths and Symbols

BIOGRAPHICAL REFERENCE

B-27   Marquis Who's Who, ed. WHO'S WHO IN AMERICA: 1978-79. 2 vols. 40th ed. Chicago: 1978.

The first volume of this standard biographical reference contains an entry (p. 950) on Mircea Eliade, noted Romanian American scholar and teacher, specialized in history of oriental religions and mythology. Main biographical data, publications, professional achievements.

MONOGRAPHS

B-28 Eliade, Mircea. BIRTH AND REBIRTH: THE RELIGIOUS MEANINGS OF INITIATION IN HUMAN CULTURE. Tr. from French by Willard R. Trask. New York: Harper and Row, 1960. 175 p.

A series of lectures on the spiritual history of humanity. Delivered by the author at the University of Chicago.

B-29 _____. FROM PRIMITIVE TO ZEN: A THEMATIC SOURCE-BOOK OF THE HISTORY OF RELIGIONS. New York: Harper and Row, 1967. 644 p.

Selections from the literature and folklore of the world intended to help students and other interested readers to understand the religious life of ancient, non-Western man. Good bibliography, but no index.

B-30 _____. IMAGES AND SYMBOLS: STUDIES IN RELIGIOUS SYMBOLISM. Tr. from French by Philip Mairet. Mission, Kansas: Sheed Andrews, 1962. 189 p.

A unique approach and contribution to the interpretation of the meaning of symbolic thinking and its importance in human existence. Scholarly and provocative.

B-31 _____. MEPHISTOPHELES AND THE ANDROGYNE: STUDIES IN RELIGIOUS MYTHS AND SYMBOL. Tr. from French by J.M. Cohen. Mission, Kans.: Sheed Andrews, 1965. 233 p.

A collection of essays confronting the old cultures of India, China, and Melanesia with Western civilization. Scholarly.

B-32 _____. MYTHS, DREAMS AND MYSTERIES: THE ENCOUNTER BETWEEN CONTEMPORARY FAITH AND ARCHAIC REALITIES. Tr. from French by Philip Mairet. New York: Harper, 1962. 236 p.

A discussion on primitive religious beliefs and their impact upon Western thought. Scholarly.

B-33 _____. OCCULTISM, WITCHCRAFT AND CULTURAL FASHION: ESSAYS IN COMPARATIVE RELIGIONS. Chicago: Chicago University Press, 1976. 148 p.

A collection of public lectures demonstrating that many modern ideas and attitudes are not the product of rationalism but of archaic religious concepts. Intended for the general reader.

B-34 _____. ZALMOXIS, THE VANISHING GOD: COMPARATIVE
STUDIES IN THE RELIGIONS AND FOLKLORE OF DACIA AND EAST-
ERN EUROPE. Tr. from French by Willard R. Trask. Chicago: Uni-
versity of Chicago Press, 1972. 260 p.

> The only scholarly book on the folklore, religions, beliefs,
> and civilizations of Dacians, ancient ancestors of Romanians,
> in comparison with the culture of their neighbors.

OTHER WORKS

B-35 Eliade, Mircea, and Kitagawa, Joseph, eds. THE HISTORY OF RELI-
GIONS: ESSAYS IN METHODOLOGY. Pref. by Gerald Brauer.
Chicago: Chicago University Press, 1961. 163 p.

> A collection of essays dealing with various aspects of method-
> ology in the field of history of religion. Scholarly.

B-36 Kitagawa, Joseph, ed. MYTHS AND SYMBOLS: STUDIES IN HONOR
OF MIRCEA ELIADE. Chicago: University of Chicago Press, 1969.
438 p.

> A collection of papers written by several scholars and students,
> most of whom were influenced by Eliade's thought.

CRITICISM

B-37 Dudley, Guilford. RELIGION ON TRIAL: MIRCEA ELIADE AND
HIS CRITICS. Philadelphia: Temple University Press, 1977. 183 p.

> A critical examination of Mircea Eliade's works. Eliade is
> presented as a moderator between two opposing camps of
> scholars: empiricists and normativists. Scholarly work.

PERIODICAL LITERATURE

B-38 Barnes, Sherman B. "Mircea Eliade's Memories." AMERICAN ROMA-
NIAN REVIEW 1 (October-November 1977): 14-16.

> Concise but very good presentation of Mircea Eliade's life,
> work, philosophy. Accompanied by Eliade's picture.

B-39 "University of Chicago Religion Professor Mircea Eliade Keeps Faith in
the Creativity of Human Spirit." PEOPLE, March 27, 1978, pp. 43-48.

> Interview with Mircea Eliade, revealing his most recent proj-
> ects, work, interests in human thought. Several pictures.

PROVERBS

B-40   Champion, Selwyn Gurney, ed. RACIAL PROVERBS: A SELECTION
OF WORLD'S PROVERBS ARRANGED LINGUISTICALLY. 2d ed. New
York: Barnes and Noble, 1963. 767 p. Index.

This comprehensive volume includes eighty-four Romanian proverbs, indicating the regions they came from. These and other
proverbs remained part of the Romanian American ethnic heritage. The translation leaves much to be desired in several
cases.

B-41   Davidoff, Henry, ed. A WORLD TREASURY OF PROVERBS FROM
TWENTY-FIVE LANGUAGES. New York: Random House, 1946.
526 p. Index.

A collection of fifteen thousand proverbs and sayings from
twenty-five languages, including Romanian, arranged by subject. The lack of an index by language makes the retrieval
of Romanian proverbs difficult.

DRAMA

Biographical Reference

B-42   Moritz, Charles, ed. CURRENT BIOGRAPHY: 1959. New York:
H.W. Wilson Co., 1959. 541 p. Index.

An extensive biography (pp. 199-211) of Eugene Ionesco,
noted Romanian playright (theater of the absurd) whose plays
RHINOCEROS, THE BALD SOPRANO, and others were successfully presented in New York theaters during the 1950s.
Although Ionesco resides in France, he often visits the United
States, and is in close touch with Romanian American intellec-
tual circles.

Collections and Criticism

B-43   Ionesco, Eugene. PLAYS. 10 vols. Tr. from French by Donald Watson.
London: J. Calder Publications, 1958-78.

The most comprehensive collection of Ionesco's plays, ranging
from THE LESSON, THE CHAIRS, and THE BALD SOPRANO
to OH, WHAT A BLOODY CIRCUS. Accompanied by Ionesco's
biography and early English criticism. See also entries B-64,
B-65.

B-44   Lamont, Rosette C., comp. IONESCO: A COLLECTION OF CRITICAL

ESSAYS. Englewood Cliffs, N.J.: Prentice-Hall, 1973. 188 p.

A critical examination of Ionesco's plays by various authors.

SHORT STORIES

Indexes—References

B-45 Cook, Dorothy E., and Monro, Isabel S., eds. THE SHORT STORY INDEX. New York: H.W. Wilson Co., 1953. 1,553 p.

This standard reference tool for 60,000 stories lists three short stories on Romanian Americans: "All in One Wild Roumanian Song" by Konrad Bercovici, "The Millionaire" by M. Asad-Weiss, and "The Greenhorn" by Peter Neagoe.

B-46 Fidell, Estelle A., ed. THE SHORT STORY INDEX. SUPPLEMENT 1969-1973. New York: H.W. Wilson Co., 1974. 639 p.

Five new short stories on Roumanian Americans are listed: "The Disciple of Bacon" by L. Epstein, "Runaway" by B.C. Green, "Rump-Titty-Titty-Tum-Tah-Tee" by F. Leiber, "Run with the Wind" by J. McKimmey, and "Rumfuddle" by J. Vance. They are mentioned under the entry "Romanians in the United States."

Collections

B-47 Neagoe, Peter. STORM: A BOOK OF SHORT STORIES. Intr. by Eugene Jolas. Paris: New Review Publications, 1932. 180 p. Pap.

A collection of short stories banned by the U.S. Bureau of Customs in 1932 as immoral. The ban was lifted two years later, but the book circulated before and after the ban, and later republished under another title. See entry B-48.

B-48 _____. WINNING A WIFE AND OTHER STORIES. Intr. by J. O'Brien. New York: Coward-McCann, 1935. 292 p.

A collection of short stories, most of naturalistic orientation. Some have an American setting, others are autobiographical, and center on Romanian peasant life and their psychology. Neagoe was the best-known Romanian American fiction writer.

Miscellaneous

B-49 Sturtevant, Donald F. PETER NEAGOE AND SOME BIBLIOGRAPHIC NOTES. Syracuse, N.Y.: Syracuse University Press, 1964. 75 p. Pap.

A selective annotated bibliography encompassing Neagoe's short stories, articles, books, unpublished manuscripts, and literary correspondence kept in the library of the Syracuse University. Also, biographical sketch.

FICTION

B-50 Dumitriu, Petru. FAMILY JEWELS. Tr. from French by Edward Hyams and Princess Anne-Marie Callimachi. New York: Pantheon Books, 1961. 437 p.

The beginning of a story devoted to the Coziano family, a powerful dynasty of Romanian boyar-aristocrats, against the background of Romania between 1862 and 1907. Although intended for the general reader, the book is of special interest to the younger generation of Romanian Americans.

B-51 _____. MEETING AT THE LAST JUDGEMENT. Tr. from French by Richard Howard. New York: Pantheon Books, 1962. 309 p.

A fictionalized version of the author's own experiences. A former director of Romania's state publishing house, Dumitriu and his wife fled to Western Europe and were forced to leave behind their baby daughter. An interesting testament of a man's protest against the abuses of a totalitarian regime, expressing the feelings of many Romanians who came to America in similar conditions.

B-52 _____. THE PRODIGALS. Tr. from French by Norman Denny. New York: Pantheon Books, 1963. 446 p.

Continuation of the Coziano family saga--the story of the fortunes of this family against the background of Bucharest society from 1914 to 1944. See entry B-50 for beginning.

B-53 Eliade, Mircea. THE FORBIDDEN FOREST. Tr. from Romanian by Mac Linscott Ricketts and Mary Park Stevenson. Notre Dame, Ind.: University of Notre Dame Press, 1978. 600 p.

A pursuit of hope for immortality through various vicissitudes during the middle of the 1930s through the middle of the 1940s. The novel is rich in themes drawn from mythology, religious and philosophical lore, and Romanian folklore. Considered by the author as his major work. See entries B-28 through B-35.

B-54 Horia, Vintila. GOD WAS BORN IN EXILE. Pref. by Daniel-Rops. Tr. from French by A. Lytton Sells. New York: St. Martin's Press, 1961. 301 p.

A poetic-religious novel of a Romanian exile who presently
lives in Switzerland. The book is loosely based on the life
of Ovid, a Latin poet banished by Emperor Augustus to Tomi,
a port on the Black Sea portion of Romania. A significant
document of our time, skilfully transposed in another era, pro-
testing totalitarian regimes that force dissident intellectuals
into exile.

B-55   Neagoe, Peter. EASTER SUN. New York: Coward-McCann, 1934.
316 p.

Along with the story of Ileana, a Romanian peasant girl of
such outstanding beauty that no man could resist her charms,
the author unfolds everyday peasant life scenes, legends, customs, folklore, religion, and picturesque speech. Neagoe is
a leading Romanian American writer.

B-56   _____. NO TIME FOR TEARS. New York: Kamin Publishers, 1958.
284 p.

A novel presenting the rich drama and folklore of Jewish
immigrant life under the shadow of the Brooklyn Bridge in
New York at the turn of the century. See also entry B-76.

B-57   _____. THERE IS MY HEART. New York: Coward-McCann, 1936.
373 p.

A story of a Romanian peasant who starts out for America,
but before leaving his native Romania gets involved in a love
affair. Like entry B-55, the book contains simple Romanian
characters.

B-58   Sandulescu, Jacques, and Gottlieb, Anie. THE CARPATHIAN CAPER.
New York: G.P. Putnam's Sons, 1975. 319 p.

Suspense novel set in Transylvania. Driven by the desire to
revenge the death of his father at the hands of the Communist
secret police, Jaques plots to steal a fabulous treasure of religious icons from a sinister monastery high in the Carpathian
Mountains. Sandulescu is a Romanian American refugee. See
also entry B-70.

B-59   Theodorescu, E.C. MERRY MIDWIFE. Boston: Houghton Mifflin Co.,
1947. 395 p.

A novel dealing with folkways and mores of the Romanian
people, typical Romanian characters, some of which were
among first-generation Romanian Americans. The book centers
on Moshica, the midwife, who touches the life of so many
and enjoys a position of importance in the countryside. Some
expressions may seem strange to English-speaking people.

AUTOBIOGRAPHIES

B-60   Carja, Ion. CANALUL MORTII: 1949-1954 [The canal of death: 1949-1954]. New York: Actiunea Romaneasca, 1974. 589 p.

This is a sequel to item B-61, describing life for political prisoners in Romanian concentration camps: forced labor, brutal treatment of detainees. Also examines the Soviet influence in the years following World War II.

B-61   _____. INTORCEREA DIN INFERN [The return from Hell]. 2 vols. Madrid, Spain: Dacia; New York: Actiunea Romaneasca, 1969-72.

Detailed account of arrest, interrogations, and life in various Romanian prisons during the years 1949-64. The author is a Romanian American, born in West Virginia, who spent ten years as a political prisoner before returning to America.

B-62   Craciunas, Silviu. THE LOST FOOTSTEPS. New York: Farrar, Straus, 1961. 318 p.

A powerful autobiographical narrative by a Romanian American anti-Communist agent. Arrested by Romanian authorities in 1949, he spent four years in prison, made a daring escape from a prison hospital, spent three years in hiding, and finally made his exit to the West.

B-63   Eliade, Mircea. NO SOUVENIRS: JOURNAL, 1957-1969. Tr. from French by Fred H. Johnson. New York: Harper and Row, 1977. 343 p. Index.

The author is a Romanian American scholar of world stature who specialized in the history of religion and mythology. In this book, he describes daily life and dreams, nostalgia, readings, comments, and encounters with contemporary personalities such as Jung, Tillich, Ionesco, and Michaux. He also shares impressions collected during numerous travels. See also entries B-28 to B-35.

B-64   Ionesco, Eugene. FRAGMENTS OF A JOURNAL. Tr. from French by Jean Stewart. New York: Grove Publishers, 1968. 150 p.

A series of impressions, dream fragments, and philosophical reflections by a well-known contemporary playwright. The book helps the reader to better understand Ionesco's plays and the theater of the absurd.

B-65   _____. PRESENT PAST, PAST PRESENT. Tr. from French by Helen R. Lane. New York: Grove Publishers, 1971. 192 p.

A personal memoir, diary, confessions, and exploration of the
self, ranging from Ionesco's childhood in Romania and life in
France during the 1940s, to events in the 1960s. Good companion to item B-64. See also entries B-42, B-43.

B-66   Neagoe, Peter. TIME TO KEEP. New York: Coward-McCann, 1949.
281 p.

Autobiographical reminiscences of the author's boyhood in a
Transylvanian village at the beginning of the twentieth century.
Written with freshness, humor, and tender feelings for the
people of the countryside, some of whom came to America with
the author. See also entries B-45, B-47.

B-67   Nimigeanu, Dimitru. HELL MOVED ITS BORDER. London: Blanford
Press, 1960. 168 p.

A poignant and revealing tale of Soviet occupation and the
courageous struggle by the author, a Romanian peasant farmer,
and his wife and daughter, to stay alive through six dreadful
years of Communist terror. It speaks for hundreds of Romanian
American immigrants who had the same fate.

B-68   Ravage, M.E. AN AMERICAN IN THE MAKING: THE LIFE STORY
OF AN IMMIGRANT. Pref. by Louise Ravage-Tresfort. New York:
Harper and Row, 1936. Repr. New York: Dover Publications, 1971.
324 p. Pap.

An autobiography documenting the transformation of a sixteen-
year-old immigrant from Romania, who never spoke English,
into a well-educated man. The detailed history of the cultural shock suffered by the young immigrant has many present-
day implications.

B-69   Sakall, Dan, and Harrington, Alan. LOVE AND EVIL: FROM A
PROBATION OFFICER'S CASEBOOK. New York: Little, Brown and
Co., 1974. 372 p.

Sakall, a Romanian American, the seventh of ten children
born on a truck farm in rural Michigan, shares his personal
experiences before and after he became probation officer in
Tucson, Arizona. He also provides some critical observations
regarding the present correctional system.

B-70   Sandulescu, Jaques. DONBAS. New York: David McKay, 1968.
217 p.

The author's experiences in a Russian slave labor camp and escape to freedom after two years (1945-47) of misery and terror.
Sandulescu's fate had been shared by many Romanian refugees
who later settled in America or Canada. See also entry B-58.

B-71   Solomon, Michael. MAGADAN. Pref. by Irving Layton. Princeton, N.J.: Auerbach Publishers, 1971. x, 243 p.

A Romanian Canadian journalist's account of his arrest in Romania by Communist authorities, his interrogation, and the subsequent seventeen years he spent in prisons and labor camps in Romania and Russia. Special attention is accorded to Magadan, a huge Russian slave labor complex.

B-72   Stan, Anisoara. THEY CROSSED MOUNTAINS. New York: William-Frederick Press, 1947. 386 p.

A Romanian American woman, noted folklorist and folk artist, describes her immigration to America during the 1920s, her contacts with early Romanian American communities, and how she popularized Romanian folk art in various parts of America during the 1930s. An important segment of the book deals with Romanian costumes, music, and folklore. Relevant illustrations.

B-73   Vasiliu, Mircea. THE PLEASURE IS MINE. New York: Harper and Row, 1955. 278 p.

A Romanian ex-diplomat's recollections narrated with a good sense of humor. After giving up his diplomatic career in Washington, Vasiliu settled in America, married a Scottish American woman and became a book illustrator and author of children's books. Illustrated by the author.

B-74   _____. WHICH WAY THE MELTING POT? Garden City, N.Y.: Doubleday, 1963. 309 p.

A continuation of Vasiliu's recollections (see entry B-73). He recounts his adventures and eventual success as an artist and writer as well as guest speaker at ladies literary groups. Written with wit and good sense of humor. Illustrated by the author. See also entry B-85.

POETRY

Biographical Reference

B-75   Kinsman, Clare, et al., eds. CONTEMPORARY AUTHORS. Vols. 37-40. Detroit: Gale Research Co., 1973. 586 p.

This well-known reference tool mentions the death of Vasile Posteuca (1912-72), noted Romanian American poet, and refers to an obituary published in the NEW YORK TIMES. See also entries B-81, B-82.

Anthologies—General

B-76   Neagoe, Peter, ed. AMERICANS ABROAD. The Hague, Netherlands: Service Press, 1932. 476 p.

A collection of poetry and prose by fifty-two American literary figures, including Ezra Pound, Gertrude Stein, and Ernest Hemingway--who alienated themselves from America and went into exile. Accompanied by short biographical sketches. Neagoe, noted Romanian American writer, sides with the exiles, went with them abroad, and edited this volume in their honor. See also entries B-45, B-47.

B-77   Novac, Nicolae. TALMACIRI DIN LIRICA AMERINDIANA [Translations from American Indian poetry]. Munich: Editura Ion Dumitru, 1977. 118 p.

A unique collection of American Indian poems translated into Romanian by a Romanian American poet of Indiana Harbor, Indiana. Accompanied by numerous illustrations and information on several Indian tribes from which the poems were collected. See also entry B-80.

B-78   Popa, Eli, ed. ROMANIA IS A SONG: A SAMPLE OF VERSE IN TRANSLATION. Cleveland: America Publishing Co., 1967. 96 p.

A selection from Romanian folk poetry, classical poets (Eminescu, Cosbuc, Alecsandri, etc.) and Romanian American poets (Novac, Posteuca) rendered into English. Accompanied by short biographical sketches of poets included in this volume.

Anthologies—Individual

B-79   Daschevici, Eglantina. MA PATRIE [My fatherland]. Chicago: Stuttgart, West Germany: W. Scrapler, 1978. 72 p. Pap.

A collection of Romanian religious, patriotic, and folk themes rendered into French by a Romanian American poetess and song writer living in Chicago.

B-80   Novac, Nicolae. ULTIMUL INVINS [The last of the vanquished]. Cleveland: America Publishing Co., 1965. 96 p. Pap.

A collection of lyrical poems by a talented Romanian American poet and cultural activist. See also entry B-77.

B-81   Posteuca, Vasile. CATAPETEASMA BUCOVINEANA [The Bucovinean altar screen]. Ill. by Nicolae Petra. Mexico City: Posteuca, 1963. 30 p. Pap.

Poems inspired by and devoted to Bucovina, a Romanian region where the poet was born. See also entry B-75.

B-82 _____. CINTECE DIN FLUER [Songs of the flute]. Cleveland: America Publishing Co., 1962. 96 p. Pap.

Nostalgic poems by a noted Romanian American poet and editor.

B-83 Theodoru, Stefan G. VERSURI [Poems]. III. by Nina Theodoru. Madrid: Theodoru, 1974. 98 p. Pap.

Lyrical poems belonging to a gifted Romanian American poet and cultural activist residing in New York City. Illustrated by the poet's wife.

CHILDREN'S LITERATURE

Fairy Tales

INDEXES

B-84 Eastman, Mary Huse, ed. INDEX TO FAIRY TALES, MYTHS AND LEGENDS. 2d ed. Boston: F.W. Faxon Co., 1926. 610 p.

This standard children's reference work includes fairy tales by Queen Elizabeth of Romania ("Legends from River and Mountain," "Real Queen's Story Book") and by Queen Marie of Romania ("Peeping Pansy"). These and other fairy tales remained part of the Romanian American cultural heritage.

Children's Books

BIOGRAPHICAL REFERENCE

B-85 Nasso, Christine, ed. CONTEMPORARY AUTHORS. Vols. 21-24. Rev. ed. Detroit: Gale Research Co., 1977. 969 p.

Short biographical sketch of Mircea Vasiliu, Romanian American author and illustrator of children's books. Lists several of his books and dates of publication (p. 899). See entries B-73, B-86 to B-93.

MONOGRAPHS

B-86 Vasiliu, Mircea. THE GOOD NIGHT, SLEEP TIGHT BOOK. New York: Golden Press, 1970. 28 p.

A book exploring various dream possibilities on the sea. Illustrated by the author.

B-87 _____. THE MERRY WIND. New York: John Day, 1967. Unpaged.

Picture book describing some things the wind might do, such as steal hats, kites, or balloons. Illustrated by the author.

B-88 _____. THE MOST BEAUTIFUL WORLD. New York: John Day, 1970. 32 p.

A contest to find the most beautiful world leads to a violent disagreement among animals. Illustrated by the author.

B-89 _____. ONCE UPON A PIRATE SHIP. New York: Golden Press, 1974. 44 p.

Adventures of a group of children who set out on a boat trip and run into a pirate ship. Illustrated by the author.

B-90 _____. ONE DAY IN THE GARDEN. New York: John Day, 1969. Unpaged.

A presentation of trees, flowers, insects, and animals for children. Illustrated by the author.

B-91 _____. WHAT'S HAPPENING? New York: Golden Press, 1970. Unpaged.

Cartoon-like illustrations and brief text describing a day's activities in the city. Illustrated by the author.

B-92 _____. THE WORLD IS MANY THINGS. New York: John Day, 1967. Unpaged.

An introduction of the five senses to children and what one can do through their use. Illustrated by the author.

B-93 _____. THE YEAR GOES AROUND. New York: John Day, 1964. 48 p.

Picture book on nature's changes. Illustrated by the author.

Children's Illustrations

BIOGRAPHICAL REFERENCE

B-94 Kingman, Lee, and Foster, Joanna, eds. ILLUSTRATORS OF CHILDREN'S BOOKS: 1957-1966. Boston: Horn Books, 1968. xvii, 295 p. Index.

A reference book with short biographies and samples of illustrators. Mircea Vasiliu's biography is included, describing his style and technique of drawing (pp. 185-86).

BOOKS WITH ILLUSTRATIONS BY MIRCEA VASILIU

B-95   Corbett, Scott. THE BIG JOKE GAME. New York: Dutton and Co., 1972. Unpaged.

Various jokes for children. Illustrations by Mircea Vasiliu.

B-96   _____. EVER RIDE A DINOSAUR? Boston: Little, Brown and Co., 1969. 113 p.

A visit to the Museum of Natural History's dinosaur exhibit. Illustrations by Mircea Vasiliu.

B-97   Gould, Linda. THE ROYAL GIRAFFE. New York: Dutton and Co., 1971. 30 p.

A giraffe sent by the king of Egypt to King Charles X of France arouses much interest in Europe. Illustrations by Mircea Vasiliu.

B-98   Hubp, Loretta Burke. QUE SERA? WHAT CAN IT BE? New York: John Day, 1970. 63 p.

Spanish riddles translated into English. Illustrations by Mircea Vasiliu.

B-99   Peare, Catherine Owens. AARON COPLAND, HIS LIFE. New York: Holt, 1969. 148 p.

Biography of a great American composer. Illustrations by Mircea Vasiliu.

B-100   Rosenberg, Sondra. ARE THERE ANY MORE AT HOME LIKE YOU? New York: St. Martin's Press, 1973. Unpaged.

A book devoted to a musically talented teenager. Illustrations by Mircea Vasiliu.

B-101   Sheehan, Ethna. FOLK AND FAIRY TALES FROM AROUND THE WORLD. New York: Dodd, Mead, 1970. 151 p.

Traditional fairy and folk tales from various countries ranging from Brazil to China. Illustrations by Mircea Vasiliu.

B-102   Sherman, Nancy S. MISS AGATHA'S LARK. Indianapolis, Ind.: Bobbs-Merrill Co., 1968. Unpaged.

A book devoted to a bird watcher. Illustrations by Mircea Vasiliu.

ROMANIAN-ENGLISH LINGUISTICS

Manuals

B-103 Cristo-Loveanu, Elie. THE ROMANIAN LANGUAGE. Pref. by Mario Pei. New York: Cristo-Loveanu, 1962. 487 p. Index.

This is the first and best manual on Romanian by a Romanian American. Encompasses phonetics, morphology, reading exercises, word formation, syntax, old and new literature, folk songs, and modern poetry. The author taught Romanian for twenty-five years at Columbia University.

B-104 Fogarassy, O. TALMACIU ROMAN ENGLEZESC COMPUS PENTRU ROMANII AFLATORI ASTAZI IN AMERICA [Romanian English interpreter compiled for the Romanians presently living in America]. Youngstown, Ohio: Fogarassy, 1905. 151 p.

One of the earliest manuals of English geared to Romanian immigrants. Interesting for research purposes.

B-105 Nandris, Grigore. COLLOQUIAL ROMANIAN: GRAMMAR, EXERCISES, READER VOCABULARY. 2d ed. New York: Dover Publications, 1953. 352 p. Index.

Consists of several parts: the Romanian alphabet and its pronunciation, spelling, grammar, syntax, reading section, and comprehensive vocabulary. Also, information on the nature of the Romanian language and its dialects. Useful to Romanian American youth and others taking Romanian language courses.

Bilingual Dictionaries

B-106 Axelrad, Philip. TALMACIU, PRONUNTATOR SI DICTIONAR ENGLEZ-ROMAN SI ROMAN-ENGLEZ [English-Romanian and Romanian-English interpreter and pronunciation dictionaries]. New York: Biblioteca Romana, 1914. 222 p.

One of the early dictionaries compiled for Romanian immigrants in America. Of interest to researchers.

B-107 Miroiu, Mihai. ENGLISH-ROMANIAN CONVERSATION BOOK. New York: Ungar Publishing Co., 1971. 199 p.

Everyday phrases covering such topics as traveling, weather, hotel, shopping, restaurants, education, and health. Although

designed for tourists, the dictionary is useful to Romanian
American students and others who want to improve their conversation skills in Romanian.

B-108 _____. ROMANIAN-ENGLISH CONVERSATION BOOK. New York:
Ungar Publishing Co., 1971. 199 p.

Has the same structure as entry B-107, but aimed at Romanians
visiting English-speaking countries. Also useful to newly
arrived Romanian immigrants interested in improving their
English, as well as to translators.

Periodical Literature

B-109 Limbeson, Mary Anne. "Americanizing the Romanian Language in the
United States." NEW PIONEER 2 (April 1944): 22-25.

A well-documented article pointing out the influence of the
American environment upon the American language, and the
influx of dozens of English words (e.g., high school, street-
car, that's right) into the Romanian day-to-day speech.

FINE ARTS

Painting

PERIODICAL LITERATURE AND PAMPHLETS

B-110 "Helen de Silaghi-Sirag." CALENDARUL CREDINTA (1974): 110-12.

Short biographical sketch of a Romanian Canadian woman
painter, her works and exhibits. Accompanied by pictures.

B-111 Popp, Fr. Nathaniel. HOLY ICONS. Detroit: Romanian Orthodox
Episcopate of America, 1972. 36 p. Pap.

A brief study devoted to the meaning, style, painting, and
use of icons in the Romanian Orthodox churches. Useful to
art students interested in icons.

Sculpture

BIOGRAPHICAL REFERENCE

B-112 Jaques Cattell Press, ed. WHO'S WHO IN AMERICAN ART: 1978.
New York: R.R. Bowker Co., 1978. 946 p. Index.

Standard reference tool. Has an entry (p.18) on Constantin

Antonovici, Romanian American sculptor, noted for his owls.
Main biographical data, important works, memberships, prizes,
and exhibits are listed. Also, museums with his works.

B-113 McGlauflin, Alice Coe, ed. THE AMERICAN ART ANNUAL (1933).
Washington, D.C.: American Federation of Arts, 1934. 848 p. Index.

Biographical sketch of George Zolnay, noted Romanian American sculptor, is included (pp. 775-76). Credited with the
Sequoyah statue in the U.S. Capitol, the Edgar Allan Poe
monument at the University of Virginia, the War Memorial,
the sculpture of the Parthenon in Nashville, Tennessee, and
several others. See also entries J-10 to J-17.

MONOGRAPHS ON CONSTANTIN BRANCUSI AND HIS WORKS

B-114 Geist, Sidney. BRANCUSI: A STUDY OF THE SCULPTURE. New
York: Grossman Publishers, 1968. 247 p. Index.

Constantin Brancusi, a Romanian sculptor of international fame,
spent a part of his life in America, where he found numerous
disciples and friends. He is well represented in leading
American museums of art as well as in private collections.
The book is based on the examination of Brancusi's works and
on a wealth of documentation. A short biography of Brancusi
is appended. Also, extensive bibliography and illustrations.

B-115 _____. BRANCUSI: THE SCULPTURE AND DRAWINGS. New York:
Harry N. Abrams, 1975. 199 p. Index.

This second book by the same author, and American authority
on Brancusi, is devoted to Brancusi's artistic evolution. It
consists of a chronology of the great artist's life, an extensive
bibliography, a documented catalog of Brancusi's sculptures,
and a unique concordance collating the sculptures cataloged
in all major books on Brancusi currently in print in the United
States and abroad. Good illustrations and plates.

B-116 Giedion-Wecker, Carola. CONSTANTIN BRANCUSI. Tr. from German
by Maria Jolas and Anne Leroy. New York: George Braziller, 1959.
240 p.

This book is considered one of the best critical analyses of
Brancusi. Consists of three parts: critical study devoted to
the main features of Brancusi's art and personality; a section
encompassing 233 plates, including Brancusi's own photographs;
and various appendixes ranging from Brancusi's maxims on art
to Brancusi's lawsuit brought in 1926 against the New York
authorities. Brancusi won the lawsuit demonstrating that his
"Golden Bird" is not just raw metal but a work of art that is

not subject to custom dues. This lawsuit became a milestone
in the history of contemporary art. Very good bibliography.

B-117 Jianou, Ionel. BRANCUSI. Pref. by Jean Cassou. New York: Tudor
Publishing Co., 1963. 223 p.

A good description of Brancusi's life and accomplishments.
Includes a catalog and illustrations of Brancusi's works, a
list of Brancusi's exhibits, chronology of events, and detailed
bibliography. The majority of illustrations reflect works acquired by American museums or private collectors.

B-118 Lewis, David. CONSTANTIN BRANCUSI. New York: St. Martin's
Press, 1974. 80 p.

A collection of illustrations of important sculptures, presently
in the hands of American private collectors and museums.
Preceded by a short biographical sketch, concise bibliography,
and biographic outline. Good for quick reference.

SPECIAL STUDIES ON CONSTANTIN BRANCUSI

B-119 Balas, Edith. "The Sculpture of Brancusi in Light of His Romanian Heritage." Ph.D. dissertation, University of Pittsburgh, 1973. 192 p.

A study dealing with the role of the Romanian artisan heritage
in Brancusi's sculpture as well as the folk art and folkloric
elements in it. Profusely illustrated with evidence of the
parallel between the architectural elements, household furnish-
ings and utensils from Brancusi's native region, and his sculpture. A special chapter is devoted to Romanian folktales,
beliefs, and metaphors underlying some of Brancusi's pieces of
sculpture.

B-120 Spear, Athena T. BRANCUSI'S BIRDS. New York: New York University Press, 1969. 152 p.

An examination of Brancusi's twenty-eight birds--marble and
bronze--from the historical, technical, and stylistic viewpoints.
With special reference to Brancusi's "Maiastra Bird" and the
influence of Romanian folklore over Brancusi's works. Includes
a chronological list of exhibitions and sales in the United
States and abroad, a biographical chronology, and an extensive bibliography.

CONSTANTIN BRANCUSI EXHIBITS

B-121 The Brummer Gallery. New York: BRANCUSI: EXHIBITION, NOVEM-
BER 17-DECEMBER 15, 1926. Pref. by Paul Morand. New York: 1926.
46 p. Pap.

An illustrated catalog of the exhibition of seventy works, including "Maiastra," "Bird in Space," "Mlle Pogany," and
other famous sculptures; thirty-two full-page illustrations, for
the most part from photographs made by Brancusi himself.
Also, maxims by Brancusi, and opinions about Brancusi by
Ezra Pound, John Quinn, Carl Sandburg, Angus Wilson, and
others.

B-122 Solomon R. Guggenheim Museum. New York: CONSTANTIN
BRANCUSI: 1976-1957, A RETROSPECTIVE EXHIBITION. Pref. by
Sidney Geist. New York: 1969. 157 p.

A catalog of the exhibition organized by the Solomon R.
Guggenheim Museum, the Philadelphia Museum of Art, and
the Art Institute of Chicago, the three main museums where
Brancusi's works can be found. Illustrations.

CONSTANTIN BRANCUSI IN PERIODICAL LITERATURE

B-123 "Brancusi: Master of Reductions." TIME, October 17, 1969, pp. 88-89.

Short presentation of some of Brancusi works. Accompanied by
illustrations.

B-124 Chanin, A.L. "Art Exhibit at Guggenheim Museum." NATION,
November 12, 1955, pp. 425-26.

Critical examination of the first major Brancusi retrospective
exhibition.

B-125 "Constantin Brancusi." AMERICAN ROMANIAN REVIEW 1 (September
1977): 4-8.

Biographical sketch of the world famous sculptor, his main
works, and American museums where he is represented. Illustrations.

B-126 Dudley, D. "Brancusi." DIAL 82 (February 1927): 123-30.

Discussion of Brancusi works after the 1926 exhibit at the
Brummer Gallery in New York City.

B-127 "Great Recluse." LIFE, December 5, 1955, pp. 131-32.

Pictures of Brancusi and some of his works.

B-128 Mamford, L. "Brancusi at the Brummer Gallery." NEW REPUBLIC,
December 15, 1926, pp. 112-13.

Critical examination of the Brancusi exhibit in 1926.

B-129 "Man in White." NEWSWEEK, November 14, 1955, p. 102.

   Pictures of Brancusi and some of his works, accompanied by comments.

B-130 "Master of the Form." TIME, November 14, 1955, pp. 88-89.

   Examination of Brancusi's exhibit at the Guggenheim Museum in 1955.

B-131 Pach, W. "Brancusi." NATION, December 1, 1926, p. 566.

   Short article on Brancusi's 1926 exhibit at the Brummer Gallery in New York City.

B-132 "People Are Still Talking About. . . ." VOGUE, October 1, 1969, pp. 40-43.

   The impact of Brancusi's retrospective exhibit at the Solomon R. Guggenheim Museum in 1955.

B-133 Saarinen, A.B. "Strange Story of Brancusi." NEW YORK TIMES MAGAZINE, October 23, 1955, pp. 26-27.

   Examination of some Brancusi works with relevant illustrations.

B-134 "Sculptor's Revenge." TIME, April 27, 1962, p. 48.

   Brancusi's picture and a short article on him.

B-135 Shirey, D.L. "Essence of Things: Display at the New York's Guggenheim Museum." NEWSWEEK, December 8, 1968, p. 137.

   Brief discussion of Brancusi's retrospective exhibit.

B-136 Soby, J.T. "Fine Arts." SATURDAY REVIEW, December 3, 1955, pp. 50-51.

   Article on Brancusi's retrospective exhibit at the Guggenheim Museum in New York. Illustrations.

B-137 Tancock, J. "Is Brancusi Still Relevant?" ART NEWS, October, 1966, pp. 40-43.

   Comments on Brancusi's exhibit at the Philadelphia Museum of Arts.

B-138 Williams, W.C. "Brancusi: First Major Retrospective Exhibition at the Solomon R. Guggenheim Museum." ARTS, November 1955, pp. 21-25.

   Ample discussion of Brancusi's exhibit, accompanied by several reproductions.

CONSTANTIN BRANCUSI OBITUARY

B-139   "Constantin Brancusi."   NEW YORK TIMES, March 16, 1957, p. 19.

Brancusi's life, works, and significance.   See also entries J-1 to J-6 of this guide.

MISCELLANEOUS

B-140 ANTONOVICI. New York: Mond'Art Galleries, 1959.   Unpaged.

A catalog describing twenty-nine works by Constantin Antonovici, Romanian American sculptor, well known for his owls. Short biography. See also entry B-112.

APPLIED ARTS

Costumes

REFERENCE—INDEXES

B-141 Monro, Isabel, and Cook, Dorothy, eds. COSTUME INDEX: A SUBJECT INDEX TO PLATES AND TO ILLUSTRATED TEXT. New York: H.W. Wilson Co., 1937. 338 p.

This standard reference book has an entry on Romanian general and regional (Bessarabia, Banat, Bucovina, Transylvania, etc.) costumes. Since Romanian Americans brought with them costumes from various regions, and some of these costumes are preserved in Romanian heritage centers or American museums, the index is very helpful for identification and documentation purposes.

B-142 Monro, Isabel, and Monro, Kate, eds. COSTUME INDEX SUPPLEMENT: A SUBJECT INDEX TO PLATES AND ILLUSTRATED TEXT. New York: H.W. Wilson Co., 1957. 210 p.

Brings up to date the former index. Has an entry on Romanian costumes, general and regional: Bucovina, Transylvania, Wallachia. Good for identification and documentation.

PERIODICAL LITERATURE

B-143 Anagnostache, Mary. "The Romanian Costume." NEW PIONEER 5 (January-April 1944): 7-9.

Good background information on Romanian costumes from different regions, accompanied by illustrations. Such costumes were preserved by Romanian immigrants and still worn during national or religious holidays.

Furniture and Interior Design

PERIODICAL LITERATURE AND PAMPHLETS

B-144 Pittsburgh. University of. Achievements of the Nationality Committees and Office of the Cultural and Educational Exchange. THE ROMANIAN CLASSROOM. Pittsburgh: University of Pittsburgh, n.d. 4 p.

   A pamphlet describing the history of the room, supporters, and the interior arrangement. Illustrations.

B-145 "The Romanian Classroom in the Cathedral of Learning, University of Pittsburgh." NEW PIONEER 1 (July-September 1943): 14-15.

   Short description of the Romanian classroom--walls, furniture, painting, architecture--officially opened on March 16, 1943, and still in existence as a monument of Romanian heritage in America.

Embroidery

PAMPHLET

B-146 Harkness, Dorothy Norris. ROMANIAN EMBROIDERY: A DYING FOLK ART. New York: Iuliu Maniu Foundation, 1960. 23 p. Pap.

   A brief but very good description of Romanian embroidery, its historical background and regional characteristics combined with technical aspects: materials, designs, stitches. The illustrations are of excellent quality. The author is a profound connoisseur of Romanian art, and active supporter of the Romanian community in New York City.

Stamps

REFERENCE—CATALOGS

B-147 SCOTT STANDARD POSTAGE STAMP CATALOGUE. 4 vols. New York: Scott Publishing Co., 1979. Index.

   Standard reference set for stamp collectors. The last volume has a section on Romanian stamps, from 1858 to our day. Of interest to collectors of Romanian stamps.

PERIODICAL LITERATURE

B-148 Partington, Paul. "A.T.A. Biography Service--Romania." TOPICAL TIME, March-April 1977, pp. 12-15.

Highlights on Romanian stamps honoring prominent personalities
in the fields of music, education, politics, and so forth.
Of interest to topical stamp collectors.

B-149 Weirich, Jerry. "The Plate Varieties of Romania." SOUTH SLAVIC
PHILATELIC MAGAZINE 1 (Winter 1977): 31-36.

An article dealing with stamps honoring King Carol I of Romania, their diversity, paper, perforations, watermarks, plates,
retouches, and errors. King Carol I was the first Romanian
monarch, and the stamps issued during his period of reign be-
long to the field of classical philately.

THEATER ARTS AND FESTIVALS

Biographical References

B-150 Moritz, Charles, ed. CURRENT BIOGRAPHY YEARBOOK: 1978.
New York: H.W. Wilson Co., 1928. 504 p. Index.

Extensive biography of Andrei Serban, young and talented
Romanian American theater director, associated with La Mama
Experimental Theater Club in New York City. Accompanied
by Serban's picture and short bibliography (pp. 376-80).

MONOGRAPH

B-151 Sickels, Alice L. AROUND THE WORLD IN ST. PAUL. St. Paul and
Minneapolis: University of Minnesota Press, 1945. 265 p.

The story of six famous festivals of nations (1932-39) held in
St. Paul, Minnesota, and the contributions made by the Romanians along with other ethnic groups. Excellent pictures
of Romanian American participants.

PERIODICAL LITERATURE

B-152 "Prima Case de Cultura in America" [The first house of culture in
America]. AMERICA, September 8, 1924, p. 1.

Short background information on the first Romanian American
house of culture, opened on August 25, 1924, in Indiana
Harbor, Indiana. In such houses, Romanian immigrants celebrated their holidays, presented plays, or held social gather-
ings.

B-153 "Teatrul Romanesc in Coloniile Noastre" [The Romanian theater in our
colonies]. AMERICA, September 18, 1923, p. 1.

Description of theatrical manifestations in several Romanian American communities.

Movies and Television

REFERENCE—HANDBOOKS AND INDEXES

B-154 Halliwell, Leslie, ed. THE FILMGOER'S COMPANION. 4th ed. New York: Avon, 1975. 1071 p.

A comprehensive and handy encyclopedic tool listing movies, actors, directors, producers, and so forth, arranged alphabetically. The entry on Jean Negulesco (p. 713), noted Romanian American movie director gives main biographical data and a listing of twenty-seven movies directed by him between 1934 and 1970.

B-155 THE NEW YORK TIMES FILM REVIEWS. Vol. 6. Appendix Index: 1913-1968. New York: New York Times, 1969.

Lists all movies directed by Jean Negulesco, ranging from THE KISS (1934) to SINGAPORE WOMAN (1941), THREE COINS IN A FOUNTAIN (1954), and THE PLEASURE SEEKERS (1964). Also, shows Negulesco's work as author, producer, and screenwriter. See also entries J-8, J-9.

PERIODICAL LITERATURE

B-156 "Director-Artist Jean Negulesco Sketches the Faces of the Stars Who Act in His Movie." LIFE, June 19, 1944, pp. 65-67.

Short biographical sketch of Jean Negulesco, movie director for Warner Brothers, accompanied by several photographs: Negulesco and Hedy Lamar, Jack Carson, Peter Lorre, Paul Henreid, and others. Negulesco's paintings and sketches were successfully exhibited in New York, Washington, Seattle, and Paris.

B-157 "John Florea--T.V. Producer and Director." NEW YORK MIRROR, August 6, 1958, p. 58.

Sheds light on John Florea's work in "Sea Hunt," a successful television series. Illustrations. See also entry A-38.

B-158 "John Florea Shooting Yellow Sky Movie." LIFE, January 10, 1949, pp. 42-49.

Several pictures presenting John Florea, noted Romanian World War II correspondent and cameraman, at work on a new movie.

Radio Broadcasting

REFERENCE—DIRECTORIES

B-159 American Council for Nationalities Service. FOREIGN LANGUAGE
RADIO STATIONS IN THE UNITED STATES. New York: American
Council for Nationalities, 1964. Unpaged. Pap.

> Lists two radio stations broadcasting Romanian programs at the
> beginning of the 1960s.

B-160 Andronescu, Serban, comp. WHO'S WHO IN ROMANIAN AMERICA.
New York: Andronescu-Wyndhill, 1976. 188 p.

> A section entitled "Romanian Radio Programs" lists all past and
> present American stations broadcasting Romanian programs (pp.
> 145-46).

B-161 Tashoff, Sol, ed. BROADCASTING YEARBOOK: 1976. Washington,
D.C.: Broadcasting Publications, 1976. Unpaged. Index.

> This standard comprehensive reference directory listing, among
> others, all foreign language programs in America and Canada,
> shows only one station, WMUZ-FM, Detroit, for Romanian
> programs. For complete information, consult entry B-160.

COMMEMORATIVE ISSUES

B-162 Varciu, Theodore, and Donev, George eds. FIFTH ANNUAL ALBUM,
WJBK ROMANIAN AMERICAN RADIO HOUR. Detroit: Romanian
American Hour, 1944. 160 p.

> Profusely illustrated with pictures of Detroit Romanians support-
> ing the radio station. Also describes Romanian organizations
> of Detroit, and presents well-known Romanian poems and music
> scores.

MUSIC AND MUSICAL FORMS

Composing

BIOGRAPHICAL REFERENCES

B-163 Slonimsky, Nicholas, ed. BAKER'S BIOGRAPHICAL DICTIONARY OF
MUSICIANS. 5th ed. New York: G. Schirmer, 1958. 1,855 p.

> This standard reference tool has an entry on George Enesco,
> world-renowned Romanian composer, who popularized Romanian

music in the United States, had been associated with several
American symphonic orchestras, and taught at the Manhattan
Mannes College. Lists tours, concerts, and major works
(pp. 438–39).

PERIODICAL LITERATURE

B-164 "Composer-Conductor-Fiddler." TIME, January 17, 1938, pp. 50–51.

Article devoted to George Enesco as performer and conductor
with the Philadelphia Orchestra. Accompanied by Enesco's
picture.

B-165 "Enesco and Menuhin." LIFE, February 6, 1950, p. 42.

Pictures and text on the friendship and collaboration between
George Enesco and Yehudi Menuhin, noted American violinist.
Enesco was Menuhin's teacher.

B-166 "George Enesco." NEW PIONEER 3 (July–September 1943): 4–6.

Short but good biographical sketch of George Enesco and his
activities as composer, violinist, pianist, and conductor.
Picture.

B-167 "George Enesco Conducts Philarmonic." MUSICIAN, February 1939,
p. 25.

Short presentation of George Enesco as guest conductor of the
Philadelphia Symphonic Orchestra.

B-168 Heyibut, R. "Building Musicianship." ETUDE, July 1949, p. 401.

An article eulogizing Enesco's talents. With biographical note.

B-169 Kaufmann, H.L. "George Enesco as I Knew Him." ETUDE, February
1956, p. 13.

An article devoted to Enesco's life and activities shortly after
the composer's death. Picture.

B-170 Milburn, F. "Fourfold Musician." MUSICAL AMERICA, January 1955,
p. 8.

Examines Enesco's talent as composer, violinist, pianist, and
conductor. Accompanied by illustrations.

B-171 "Obituaries." ETUDE, July 1955, p. 7; NEW YORK TIMES, May 5, 1955,
p. 33; NEWSWEEK, May 16, 1955, p. 76; TIME, May 15, 1955, p. 93.

These notices shed light on Enesco's life and development as musician of international stature, activities and concerts in America, as well as main works. Pictures. See also entry J-7.

Conducting

BIOGRAPHICAL REFERENCE

B-172 Ewen, David, ed. LIVING MUSICIANS. 1st supplement. New York: H.W. Wilson Co., 1957. 178 p.

This popular reference work includes the biography of Ionel Perlea, noted Romanian American conductor at the Metropolitan Opera of New York (pp. 122-23). Accompanied by picture.

PERIODICAL LITERATURE

B-173 "Ionel Perlea." METRO OPERA NEWS, December 12, 1949, pp. 4-5, 24.

Extensive biography of Ionel Perlea, his activities as conductor at the New York Metropolitan Opera and teacher at Manhattan College of Music. Picture.

B-174 "Obituary." NEW YORK TIMES, July 31, 1970, p. 30.

Short biography of Ionel Perlea, outlining main aspects of his life and musical profession. Latest picture.

Performing

PERIODICAL LITERATURE

B-175 Hughes, Allen. "Marioara Trifan, Gifted Pianist, Is Heard in Her New York Debut." NEW YORK TIMES, March 11, 1972, p. 16.

Short biographical sketch of Marioara Trifan, a gifted Romanian American pianist from New Jersey, who graduated from the Juilliard School, started to appear in public concerts at the age of eleven, and earned several prizes abroad. Picture.

Opera

PERIODICAL LITERATURE

B-177 Kaplan, Arthur. "Aida Was Her Signature Role." SAN FRANCISCO OPERA MAGAZINE (1977): 20-24.

The most recent interview with Stella Roman, noted Romanian American dramatic soprano, at the New York Metropolitan Opera and at the San Francisco Opera between 1940 and 1951. Accompanied by several pictures of Stella Roman as Aida, La Gioconda, and from private life.

B-178 "Stella Roman." NEW PIONEER 1 (April 1943): 6; 4 (April 1946): 27.

Short presentations of Stella Roman, a celebrated soprano at the New York Metropolitan Opera, who made her debut as Aida. Shows her support for the Romanian American community through benefit concerts.

Folk Music

ANTHOLOGIES

B-179 Smarandescu, Nicolae, comp. CINTECE SI MELODII ROMANESTI [Romanian folk songs and tunes]. Detroit: Romanian Orthodox Episcopate of America, 1972. 112 p. Pap.

This is the first collection of Romanian folk music--popular songs, tunes, carols, and choir music for solos, duets, instruments--put together in this country. Indexes musical notes and Romanian-language text. Designed for Romanian American youth and community groups interested in the preservation of Romanian heritage in America and Canada.

B-180 Tomulet, John, comp. COLINDE DE CRACIUN [Christmas carols.]. Detroit: Romanian Orthodox Episcopate of America, 1972. 112 p. Pap.

A selection of one hundred most popular Romanian Christmas carols, with music and Romanian words, designed for youth groups in America and Canada.

PERIODICAL LITERATURE

B-181 Ocneanu, Traian. "The Doina-Romanian Folk Song." NEW PIONEER 1 (July-September 1943): 16-17.

Description of the Doina, Romania's most popular folk song, and its character. Accompanied by notes.

Recorded Music

PERIODICAL LITERATURE

B-182 "Romanian Music." NEW PIONEER 2 (July 1943): 56; Reprinted in

AMERICAN ROMANIAN REVIEW 2 (May-June 1978): 14.

Lists records of Romanian music produced by Columbia, Decca,
and Victor record companies: Enesco's rhapsodies played by
American symphonic orchestras, concerts by Enesco and
Menuhin, violin performances by Dinicu and Heifetz, Romanian
popular melodies. Each record title is accompanied by identification number of the company and short annotation. Of
interest to record collectors and libraries.

FOLK DANCING

Periodical Literature

B-183 "Hora Mare." NEW PIONEER 5 (January-April 1947): 10-14.

Good presentation of the Hora Mare (great dance), a Romanian
popular dance performed in circle symbolizing national unity.
With musical notes, diagram of steps, and full explanation of
movements.

C. SOCIAL SCIENCES

IMMIGRATION AND SETTLEMENT IN AMERICA AND CANADA, GENERAL

Reference—Handbooks

C-1   Miller, Wayne Charles, ed. A COMPREHENSIVE BIBLIOGRAPHY FOR THE STUDY OF AMERICAN MINORITIES. 2 vols. New York: New York University Press, 1976. Index.

> Covers several ethnic American groups including the Romanians. Despite the title, the Romanian Americans are treated superficially--only a one-page introductory essay (erroneously considering the Romanians as Slavs) and an annotated bibliography with thirty-three items, but incomplete (vol. 1, pp. 675-76). The weakest sections: periodicals, autobiographies, and fiction.

C-2   _____. A HANDBOOK OF AMERICAN MINORITIES. New York: New York University Press, 1976. 225 p.

> A condensed version of entry C-1. Romanian Americans are treated very succintly and superficially--just one page with a few citations and the statement that the Romanians are Slavs, disregarding their Latin background (p. 143). Could be used for quick reference only.

C-3   Wertsman, Vladimir, ed. THE ROMANIANS IN AMERICA: 1748-1974. A CHRONOLOGY AND FACT BOOK. Ethnic Chronology Series, no. 19. Dobbs Ferry, N.Y.: Oceana Publications, 1975. vi, 118 p. Index.

> Compact handbook destined for high school and community college students. Consists of a chronological section, documents, annotated bibliography, and appendixes listing organizations, periodicals and art collections, statistical tables. Bibliography has thirty-six items leading to further research.

Social Sciences

General Studies

C-4   Brown, Francis, and Roucek, Joseph S., eds. ONE AMERICA: THE
       HISTORY, CONTRIBUTIONS, AND PRESENT PROBLEMS OF OUR
       RACIAL AND NATIONAL MINORITIES. 2d ed. New York: Prentice-
       Hall, 1945. xvi, 716 p. Index.

       In this revised edition of the previous book, the chapter on
       Romanian Americans (pp. 223-32) was written by Francis Brown,
       shortened, and updated with materials from the NEW PIONEER.
       The bibliography was partly changed. Good for historical re-
       search.

C-5   _____. ONE AMERICA: THE HISTORY, CONTRIBUTIONS, AND
       PRESENT PROBLEMS OF OUR RACIAL AND NATIONAL MINORITIES.
       3d ed. Englewood Cliffs, N.J.: Prentice-Hall, 1952. xvi, 764 p.
       Index.

       The Romanian American chapter (pp. 227-31) of this new edi-
       tion has been again changed and shortened by Peter Trutza,
       a noted Romanian American leader. New immigration statistics
       were added, and the bibliography partly modified. Still useful
       for quick reference leading to further research.

C-6   _____. OUR RACIAL AND NATIONAL MINORITIES: THEIR HISTORY,
       CONTRIBUTIONS AND PRESENT PROBLEMS. New York: Prentice-
       Hall, 1937. xxi, 874 p. Index.

       One of the first comprehensive studies devoted to several ethnic
       American groups. The chapter on Romanian Americans (pp.319-30)
       was written by Christine Avghi Galitzi, author of entry C-9.
       It deals with the historical background of Romanian Americans,
       geographical distribution, cultural differentiation and assimila-
       tion, religion, press, organizations, and contributions to
       America. Good for historical research. Bibliography.

C-7   Drutzu, Serban. ROMANII IN AMERICA [The Romanians in America].
       Chicago: Tipografia S. Alexandru, 1922. 207 p.

       This is the first book on Romanians in America and Canada by
       a Romanian American. The first part deals with causes of
       immigration, geographical distribution, occupations, social
       life, religion, press, and contributions. The second part is
       concerned with the relationship between Romanian immigrants
       and their native land. Good source of information on early
       Romanian American life. Illustrations.

C-8   Drutzu, Serban, and Popovici, Andrei. ROMANII IN AMERICA [The
       Romanians in America]. Pref. by Prof. N. Iorga. Bucharest: Cartea
       Romaneasca, 1926. 324 p.

An enlarged edition of entry C-7. Offers an in-depth and more comprehensive study on Romanian immigrants in America and Canada. A special chapter deals with practical advice for immigrants or prospective immigrants (e.g., travel papers, customs regulations, English language). Better pictures than in previous edition. Good source of information, but lacks bibliography and index.

C-9   Galitzi, Christine Avghi. A STUDY OF ASSIMILATION AMONG THE ROUMANIANS IN THE UNITED STATES. New York: Columbia University Press, 1929. 282 p. Index.

Basic source of information. Full and substantial coverage of the character and number of Romanian immigrants; home background; distribution in the United States; living conditions; religious, cultural, and social life, organizations; press; old culture versus new environment; trends of assimilation; persistence of ethnic contracts, and case histories of first- and second-generation Romanian Americans. Very extensive bibliography (pp. 256-72).

C-10   Iorga, Nicolae. AMERICA SI ROMANII DIN AMERICA: NOTE DE DRUM SI CONFERINTE [America and the Romanians in America: Travel notes and speeches]. Valenii-de-Munte, Romania: Asezamantul Tipografic Datian Romaneasca, 1930. 234 p.

The author, a world-famous Romanian historian, shares his impressions about America and Romanian American communities after visiting Washington, Chicago, Cleveland, Detroit, San Francisco, Los Angeles, Baltimore, Philadelphia, Boston, and other cities at the end of the 1920s. Good for historical research.

C-11   Podea, Ion. ROMANII DIN AMERICA [The Romanians of America]. Sibiu, Romania: Tipografia Archidecezana, 1912. 88 p. Pap.

One of the first comprehensive studies on Romanian Americans, dealing with early immigration, economic situation, organizations, churches, press, and cultural manifestations. The author was a Romanian Orthodox priest, organizer of the first parishes in America and Canada.

C-12   Schiopul, Iosif I. ROMANII DIN AMERICA, O CALATORIE DE STUDII IN S.U.A. [The Romanians in America, a study trip to the U.S.A.]. Sibiu, Romania: Tipografia W. Krafft, 1913. 64 p. Pap.

A description of Romanian American communities established in Illinois, Michigan, New York, Ohio, and Pennsylvania at the beginning of the twentieth century, including churches, press, cultural aspects, and adjustment to the new environment.

The author was a Romanian journalist from Transylvania, at that time under Hungarian rule.

C-13 U.S. Commissioner of Immigration. DICTIONARY OF RACES OR PEOPLES: THE ROUMANIANS. Washington, D.C.: Government Printing Office, 1907. 150 p. Pap.

Excerpt from the fifth volume of the U.S. Immigration Commission Reports. Besides including the land of origin, historical, cultural, social and political conditions, the book deals with causes of immigration, situation of Romanian immigrants in America, geographical distribution, occupations, salaries, literacy, and adjustment to the new environment.

Periodical Literature

C-14 Anagnostache, George. "Romanians in America." NEW PIONEER 2 (July 1944): 12-16.

Short presentation of the Romanian American community: size, composition, geographic distribution. Based on the 1940 U.S. Census data and immigration statistics. The author was Romania's consul in Cleveland and subsequently became an American citizen. Charts.

C-15 Galitzi, Christine A[vghi]. "The Romanians in America." ROUMANIA, July 1929, pp. 56-59.

Short but well-written article by the first Romanian American woman to gain a doctoral degree on the subject of Romanian Americans. See entry C-9.

C-16 _____. "The Romanians in America." AMERICA, August 31, 1933, p. 2.

Short background information on Romanian Americans at the beginning of the 1930s.

C-17 Popovici, Andrei. "The Romanians in America." ROUMANIA, April 1929, pp. 75-78.

Concise presentation of the Romanian American community by the author of a book on the same subject. See entry C-8.

C-18 "Roumanians in America." LITERARY DIGEST, October 11, 1919, p. 41.

A brief survey on Romanian Americans, covering number, settlement, places of concentration, immigration flow, and organizations. Prepared as a lesson in patriotism, and especially designed for school use.

C-19 Stanculescu, George. "Viata Romaneasca din America" [The Romanian life in America]. CALENDARUL NATIONAL AL ZIARULUI AMERICA (1925): 33-179.

> Extensive and well-documented study on the Romanian American community, its ethnic life and preservation of ethnic heritage.

IMMIGRATION AND SETTLEMENT IN AMERICA, REGIONAL

Illinois

MONOGRAPHS

C-20 Rex, Frederick. "The Romanian Population in Chicago." Chicago: Municipal Library. 1926. np.

> A communication paper presented by a former librarian of the Chicago Municipal Library. Based on data collected by the author.

C-21 Trutza, Peter. "The Religious Factor in Acculturation: A Study in Assimilation and Acculturation of the Roumanian Group in Chicago." Ph.D. dissertation, University of Chicago, 1956. 131 p.

PERIODICAL LITERATURE

C-22 Bohar, N. "Printre Romanii din Chicago" [Among the Romanians of Chicago]. AMERICA, August 2, 1927, p. 1.

> Short article on the Romanian community in Chicago.

Minnesota

PERIODICAL LITERATURE

C-23 Stefan, John. "The Romanians in South St. Paul, Minnesota." NEW PIONEER 3 (January 1945): 42-51.

> Well-documented article regarding the history, early settlers, and the role of Swift's and Armour's companies in attracting new immigrants. Also covers Romanian organizations, church development, youth clubs, occupations, and leaders.

Montana

PERIODICAL LITERATURE

C-24 "Romanii din Montana" [The Romanians of Montana]. CALENDARUL

ZIARULUI ROMANUL (1909): 98-100.

A more detailed article on the Romanian immigrants of Montana, including causes of immigration.

C-25   "Romanii din St. Louis, Montana" [The Romanians of St. Louis, Montana].
AMERICA, January 14, 1912, p. 2.

Short background information on the Romanian shepherds of Montana.

New York

MONOGRAPH

C-26   Bercovici, Konrad. AROUND THE WORLD IN NEW YORK. New York: Century Co., 1924. 416 p.

Description of various ethnic groups in New York City, including the Romanians, their community, residence neighborhoods and streets, coffee houses, press, library, restaurants, and theaters. Also covers relations with other ethnic groups who came from Romania.

PERIODICAL LITERATURE

C-27   Hategan, Rev. Fr. Vasile. "Romanians of New York City." NEW PIONEER 3 (April 1945): 28-50.

Extensive and very well documented article on Romanians in New York City: statistics, distribution, occupations, restaurants, bank agencies, participation during World War II, contributions to the 1939 New York World Fair, religious life, periodicals, associations, contributions to America. Excellent for researchers. The author is a noted Romanian American religious leader, social activist, and writer.

Ohio

MONOGRAPHS AND STUDIES

C-28   Andrica, Theodore, ed. ROMANIAN AMERICANS AND THEIR COMMUNITIES OF CLEVELAND. Cleveland: Cleveland State University, Ethnic Heritage Studies, 1977. 218 p.

A collection of essays revealing the history, life-style, and numerous contributions made by Romanians in Cleveland, a city once considered the metropolis of Romanian Americans. The author is a noted journalist, former editor of the NEW

PIONEER, and presently editor of the AMERICAN ROMANIAN REVIEW.

C-29   Barton, Josef J. PEASANTS AND STRANGERS: ITALIANS, RUMANI-ANS AND SLOVAKS IN AN AMERICAN CITY, 1890-1950. Cambridge, Mass.: Harvard University Press, 1975. 217 p. Index.

A study devoted to Romanians along with other ethnic groups in Cleveland. Sheds light on the origins, migration, settlement, trends in social mobility, family, and education, and compares the second with the first generation. Statistical tables and bibliographical notes. Good for researchers.

C-30   Bercovici, Konrad. ON NEW SHORES. New York: Century Co., 1925. 302 p.

A book on various ethnic groups who settled in America. The chapter on Romanian immigrants includes a brief description of the land of origin, and presentation of various Romanian families in Ohio, Michigan, and North Dakota.

C-31   Motok, Eugenia Cornea. "Roumanians in Cleveland." Master's thesis, Ohio State University, 1936. 71 p.

Based on research of 202 Romanian families who settled in Cleveland.

PERIODICAL LITERATURE

C-32   Andrica, Theodore. "The Romanians in Canton." NEW PIONEER 1 (April 1944): 23-33.

Detailed and very good study on a Romanian settlement in Canton, Ohio: early history, religious life, organizations, occupations, and names of settlers.

C-33   _____. "The Romanians in Lorain, Ohio." NEW PIONEER 1 (September 1943): 56-58.

Short but very well documented article on the history and development of the Romanian community in Lorain, Ohio.

C-34   _____. "The Romanians of the Mahoning Valley." NEW PIONEER 1 (February 1943): 26-39.

An extensive article covering the history, accomplishments, social and religious life, business, leaders, and other aspects regarding the Romanian communities in Youngstown, Warren, and Niles, Ohio.

C-35   Pascu, C.R.   "Viata Romaneasca din America" [The Romanian life in America].   AMERICA, April 10, 1913, p. 1.

     Short background information on the Romanian community of Bridgeport, Ohio.

C-36   Popescu, Aureliu.   "Colonia Romana din Cleveland" [The Romanian colony of Cleveland].   AMERICA, May 9, 1929, pp. 1-2.

     Description of the Romanian community in Cleveland, its social life and Romanian heritage.

Pennsylvania

PERIODICAL LITERATURE

C-37   Popovici, Andrei.   "Romanii din Philadelphia" [The Romanians in Philadelphia].   AMERICA, December 22, 1922, p. 2.

     Short background information on the Romanian community of Philadelphia.

C-38   "Romanii din McKees Rocks" [The Romanians of McKees Rocks]. AMERICA, May 23, 1915, p. 1.

     Sheds light on the Romanian community shortly after immigration to America.

Macedo-Romanians

C-39   "Romanii Macedoneni in America" [Macedonian Romanians in America]. AMERICA, September 28, 1906, p. 2.

     Earliest information on the background of Macedonian Romanians, a group which immigrated from Macedonia, presently divided between Greece and Albania. This group speaks a special dialect, and settled mainly in Rhode Island and New York state.

C-40   Stoica, Vasile.   "Romanii Macedoneni din America" [The Macedonian Romanians of America].   CALENDARUL AMERICA (1933): 142-44.

     Background information on immigration, settlement, organizations, and spiritual life in America.

IMMIGRATION AND SETTLEMENT IN CANADA, REGIONAL

Periodical Literature

C-41   Johnson, Gilbert.   "The Romanians in Western Canada."   SASKATCHE-

WAN HISTORY 14 (Spring 1961): 64-70.

> Historical background on the Romanian Canadian community, estimated around 15,000 at the beginning of the 1960s, and the way it preserved ethnic heritage values: national costumes, and birth, wedding, and holiday customs. Illustrations.

C-42   "Romanians in Canada." AMERICAN ROMANIAN REVIEW 2 (July-August 1978): 20-22.

> Short information on Romanian Canadian immigration, settlement, churches. Picture of the first Romanian Canadian church.

C-43   Toma, Mike G. "From Boian, Bucovina to Boian, Alberta." CALENDARUL CREDINTA (1974): 102-4.

> The beginning of Romanian immigration to Canada, and development of a Romanian colony called Boian, same name as the village where the first settlers came from. Relevant pictures.

EARLY IMMIGRANT LIFE

General Studies

C-44   Roberts, Peter. THE NEW IMMIGRATION: A STUDY OF THE INDUSTRIAL AND SOCIAL LIFE OF SOUTHEASTERN EUROPEANS IN AMERICA. New York: Macmillan Co., 1920. 560 p. Index.

> An examination of various immigrant groups, including the Romanians, their capabilities and efficiency in metallurgic and mine industries of Northern America.

C-45   Tifft, Wilton, ed. ELLIS ISLAND. Text by Thomas Dune. Illus. by Mila Macek. New York: Norton Publishing Co., 1971. Unpaged.

> A pictorial history of various immigrant groups, including the Romanians. Accompanied by short description of their arrival, immigration procedures, life on Ellis Island.

Periodical Literature

C-46   "The Boarding House." NEW PIONEER 3 (January 1945): 6-7.

> An article bringing to light the role of the boarding house in the life of early Romanian immigrants. Types of boarding houses, food, and social life, are described.

C-47   "The Saloon." AMERICAN ROMANIAN REVIEW 1 (July 1977): 26-27.

> The role early saloons--established by Romanian settlers at the turn of our century--have played in the social life of immigrants.

FOLKLORE AND POPULAR CUSTOMS—GENERAL

Periodical Literature and Pamphlets

C-48   Bucur, Nicholas A.   "What Price Romanian Customs?"   NEW PIONEER
6 (April 1948):   22-24; (June-September 1948):   25-26.

> Discusses the values of Romanian customs as preserved by the
> older generation, versus the trends of the younger generation
> born in America.   Author believes that the Romanian customs
> are good and deserve to be preserved.

C-49   Dunham, Donald C.   THE OLD COUNTRY'S CULTURAL RESPONSIBILITY
IN THE UNITED STATES.   New York: Iuliu Maniu Foundation, 1960.
16 p.   Pap.

> Appeal for a better preservation of Romanian customs and heri-
> tage in the United States, and improvement of cultural relations
> between the United States and Romania.   The author is a non-
> Romanian American who specialized in Romanian arts.

C-50   Hurgoi, Vasile.   "The New Romanian Immigrants."   AMERICAN ROMA-
NIAN REVIEW   2 (May-June 1978):   18-19.

> Short background information on Romanian immigrants during the
> last few years.   Unlike the older immigrants, only a minor part
> of the newly arrived express interest in Romanian customs and
> heritage in this country.

C-51   Limbeson, Mary Anne.   "Present Day Romanian Customs in America."
NEW PIONEER 2 (January 1944):   8-11.

> Informative article based on first-hand information.   Describes cus-
> toms brought to America and the influence of the new environment.
> Religious forms are mostly preserved in baptism, marriage, and
> funerals as well as during Christmas and Easter holidays.

C-52   Romcea, Charles.   "The Romanian American."   NEW PIONEER   4 (October 1946):   13-15.

> Discusses the place of the Romanian group in the American
> multiethnic society, the transformation it suffers.   The Roma-
> nian Americans should use their ancestral customs and heritage
> and appreciate old values.

FOLKLORE AND POPULAR CUSTOMS—AMERICAN

Periodical Literature

C-53   "Cintecul Ciobanului" [The shepherd's song].   ROMANUL, January 19,
1913, p. 6.

Popular song, with words and music by a Romanian immigrant shepherd who settled in New Mexico.

C-54 "D-ale Noastre din America" [On our way in America]. AMERICA, April 27, 1911, p. 4; June 1, 1911, p. 6; July 13, 1911, p. 5; August 24, 1911, p. 5; October 12, 1911, p. 5; November 12, 1911, p. 4.

A column reflecting various Romanian folklore creations and manifestations on American soil. Of special interest to researchers studying early Romanian American folklore.

C-55 "Doine din America" [Doinas of America]. ROMANUL, December 5, 1908, pp. 5-6.

Several Romanian popular songs called Doine, with words and music by different Romanian immigrants who came to America at the beginning of the twentieth century.

Christmas Customs

PERIODICAL LITERATURE

C-56 Ocneanu, Traian. "Christmas Caroling and Other Romanian Customs." NEW PIONEER 2 (January 1944): 23-25.

Description of customs brought from Transylvania to America, and preserved in great part, to this day.

Easter Customs

PERIODICAL LITERATURE

C-57 "First Romanian Easter in Cleveland." NEW PIONEER 1 (April 1945): 15.

A description based on the recollections of Nicholas Milhaltian, a Romanian American who settled in Cleveland at the turn of the century.

C-58 Popa-Deleu, Aurelia. "The Easter Egg." NEW PIONEER 2 (April 1944): 31-34.

Article devoted to the origin of the colored Easter eggs, the way they are colored and decorated by Romanians, styles and instruments of decoration. Accompanied by several Easter egg designs.

C-59 Popa-Deleu, John. "Easter in Romania." NEW PIONEER 1 (April 1945): 5-6.

A description of the better-known Easter customs, most of
which are still practiced in the United States. The author is
a Romanian American who came to America in the 1940s and
earned a Ph.D. from Harvard University.

Wedding Customs

PERIODICAL LITERATURE

C-60   Porea, Cornelia. "Wedding in Youngstown." NEW PIONEER 1 (February 1943): 43-45.

The author describes the wedding of her parents, both Romanian immigrants who settled in Youngstown, Ohio, at the
beginning of the twentieth century. Interesting aspects of the
old country's customs and the influence of the environment.

Folktales

MONOGRAPH

C-61   Ure, Jean, ed. RUMANIAN FOLKTALES. Illus. by Charles Mozley.
New York: Franklin Watts, 1962. 194 p.

A selection of well-told, enjoyable folk tales, many of which
were brought by Romanian immigrants and narrated to their
children and grandchildren.

EDUCATION

Biographical Reference

C-62   Jaques Cattell Press, ed. DIRECTORY OF AMERICAN SCHOLARS. 4
vols. 7th ed. New York: R.R. Bowker Co., 1978.

Standard reference tool. Includes a biographical entry of
Vasile C. Barsan, a Romanian American educator, presently
professor at Mankato State University, Minnesota (vol. 3, p.
28). Professional activities, writings, and membership.

Periodical Literature

C-63   "Early Romanian Students in America." AMERICAN ROMANIAN RE-
VIEW 2 (March-April 1978): 10-11.

A list of Romanian students attending American colleges and
universities in 1926, including a list of Romanian high schools.
Romanian American parents took exceptional pride when their
children completed high school and continued college studies.

C-64   "Prof. Charles V. Romcea." AMERICA, August 3, 1978, pp. 1-2.

   Biographical sketch of Charles V. Romcea, a noted Romanian
   American educator, principal of a high school, from Cleveland.
   The sketch was published on the occasion of Romcea's retire-
   ment. Picture.

C-65   "Studenti Romani Aflati in Colegiile si Universitatile Americane" [Roma-
   nian students in American colleges and universities]. CALENDARUL
   AMERICA (1931): 162-64.

   Lists of Romanian college and university students at the beginning of the 1930s.

C-66   "Studenti Romani la Universitatea din Pittsburgh" [Romanian students at
   Pittsburgh University]. AMERICA, May 2, 1929, p. 1.

   Listing of Romanian students attending courses at Pittsburgh University.

C-67   "Tinerii Romani Aflati in Liceele Americane in 1930" [Romanian students
   in American high schools in 1930]. CALENDARUL AMERICA (1931):
   188-93.

   Lists of Romanian high school students from various states.

SPORTS

Reference—Encyclopedia

C-68   THE BASEBALL ENCYCLOPEDIA: THE COMPLETE AND OFFICIAL RECORD
   OF MAJOR LEAGUE BASEBALL. New York: Macmillan Co., 1969.
   2,337 p.

   Well-known reference tool. Lists Charles Stanceu of Canton,
   Ohio, and his performances for the New York Yankees
   (p. 1516). Stanceu was the first Romanian American to have
   a contract with the New York Yankees during the 1941-46
   period.

Periodical Literature

C-69   Jares, Joe. "USF Wins One for the U.N." SPORTS ILLUSTRATED,
   December 12, 1966, pp. 24-25.

   Presentation of the San Francisco soccer team and its coach
   Steve Negoesco, a Romanian American teacher of biology in
   a junior high school.

ECONOMICS

Monographs

C-70 Georgescu-Roegen, Nicholas. ANALYTICAL ECONOMICS: ISSUES
AND PROBLEMS. Cambridge, Mass.: Harvard University Press, 1966.
434 p. Index.

Scholarly book discussing ideas of great thinkers in philosophy,
mathematics, and science, in an attempt to bridge the gap
between economics and science. The author is a noted Romanian American economist, whose views had a profound impact
upon American economic thinking and research.

C-71 _____. THE ENTROPY LAW AND THE ECONOMIC PROCESS. Cambridge, Mass.: Harvard University Press, 1972. 475 p. Index.

A remarkable critical analysis of economic philosophy. Man
must learn to ration his meager resources in order to survive in
the long run, because the earth is entropically winding down
naturally, and economic advance is accelerating this process.
Had great impact upon economists and scientists in America
and abroad.

Periodical Literature

C-72 "Georgescu Wins National Honor." VANDERBILT UNIVERSITY ALUMNI
OFFICE 11 (February 1972): 1.

Short biography of Professor Nicholas Georgescu-Roegen, Distinguished Professor of Economics and Distinguished Fellow of
the American Economic Association. He settled in America
in 1947, taught at Harvard University, and then joined the
faculty of Vanderbilt University. Picture.

POLITICAL SCIENCE

Monographs

C-73 Barbu, Zevedei. DEMOCRACY AND DICTATORSHIP: THEIR PSYCHOL-
OGY AND PATTERNS OF LIFE. New York: Grove Press, 1956. viii,
275 p.

A sociopsychological study examining the characteristics and
motivation of fascism, communism, and democracy. Of interest to students of political history. The author is a former
Romanian diplomat who opted to remain in the West.

C-74 Cretzianu, Alexandre, ed. CAPTIVE ROMANIA: A DECADE OF SO-
VIET RULE. New York: Praeger, 1956. xvi, 424 p.

A collection of essays by various authors regarding the negative effects of Soviet occupation, and Romania's transformation into a Soviet satellite in the first decade after World War II. The editor is a former Romanian diplomat, leader of Romanian refugees and exile groups in America and other countries.

Periodical Literature and Pamphlets

C-75 Alroy, G.C., and Abramson, M. "Escape to Freedom." CORONET 49 (February 1961): 45-50.

An article devoted to the plight of Romanian refugees opposing the Communist regime. Accompanied by pictures.

C-76 CALENDARUL ZIARULUI ROMANUL AMERICAN, 1949 [The almanac of the newspaper Romanian American, 1949]. Detroit: 1949. 288 p. Pap.

Pro-Communist publication, euologizing Romania under Communist rule and criticizing the American system.

C-77 PROSECUTION OF RELIGION IN RUMANIA. Washington, D.C.: Rumanian National Committee, 1949. 37 p. Pap.

Anti-Communist pamphlet issued by an organization of Romanian refugees and exiles in America.

C-78 SUPPRESSION OF HUMAN RIGHTS IN RUMANIA. Washington, D.C.: Rumanian National Committee, 1949. 163 p. Pap.

Anti-Communist study issued by an organization of Romanian refugees and exiles in America.

LAW

Bibliography

C-79 Stoicoiu, Virgiliu. LEGAL SOURCES AND BIBLIOGRAPHY OF ROMANIA. New York: Frederick A. Praeger, 1964. 237 p. Index.

Annotated bibliography of legal writings. It is the first of its kind to be published in English and Romanian, and written by a Romanian refugee under the auspices of the Library of Congress. Preceded by an introduction to Romanian law.

Periodical Literature

C-80 "Ceva Despre Legile Americane" [Something about the American laws]. CALENDARUL ROMANUL (1909): 17-33.

Condensed and popular presentation of American laws for newly arrived Romanian immigrants

STATISTICS

Census Reports (in chronological order)

C-81   U.S. Department of Commerce. Bureau of the Census. THE TWELFTH CENSUS OF THE UNITED STATES IN THE YEAR 1900. 10 vols. Washington, D.C.: Government Printing Office, 1901-2.

Various ethnic groups, including Romanians, who immigrated to the United States were recorded under the heading "Foreign Stock" in the volumes dealing with population composition and characteristics. The census date coincides with the beginning of Romanian mass immigration to America, but the immigrants were recorded by country of birth (e.g., Austro-Hungary, Romania), regardless of ethnic background. To sort out the Romanian ethnics from such data has been and remains a difficult problem for researchers.

C-82   _____. THE THIRTEENTH CENSUS OF THE UNITED STATES IN THE YEAR 1910. 15 vols. Washington, D.C.: Government Printing Office, 1911-13.

In addition to the country of birth, the census recorded the spoken language of the immigrants and their children. The Romanian ethnic group is better identifiable than in the previous census. Also, there is a geographic distribution of Romanian immigrants by state.

C-83   _____. THE FOURTEENTH CENSUS OF THE UNITED STATES IN THE YEAR 1920. 15 vols. Washington, D.C.: Government Printing Office, 1921-23.

Data regarding the Romanians are similar to those encountered in the previous census: country of birth, spoken language of immigrants and their children, sex, and geographical distribution in America.

C-84   _____. THE FIFTEENTH CENSUS OF THE UNITED STATES IN THE YEAR 1930. 32 vols. Washington, D.C.: Government Printing Office, 1931-33.

This census incorporated new data on Romanian ethnics: citizenship, naturlization, literacy, age groups, year of immigration, marital status, level of assimilation, geographical distribution by state, proportion between rural and urban areas, and other aspects. However, newborn babies were ·recorded as Americans regardless of ethnic background.

C-85 _____. THE SIXTEENTH CENSUS OF THE UNITED STATES IN THE YEAR 1940. 48 vols. Washington, D.C.: Government Printing Office, 1941-43.

> Contains data similar to those taken during the previous census. It coincides with the first years of World War II, when the Romanian immigration to America went sharply down, reaching the lowest level in the last four decades.

C-86 _____. CENSUS OF POPULATION, 1970. SUBJECT REPORTS: NATIONAL ORIGIN AND LANGUAGE. Washington, D.C.: Government Printing Office, 1973. 505 p.

> Like all other previous censuses, this one recorded the Romanians as well as other ethnic groups, by place of birth and spoken language. Such a criterion complicates the identification of Romanian ethnics because Romania was the country of birth of several ethnic groups: Hungarians, Germans, Jews, Armenians, Greeks, and others who immigrated to America, but do not belong to the Romanian ethnic community.

Abstracts and Other Sources

C-87 U.S. Department of Commerce. Bureau of the Census. STATISTICAL ABSTRACT OF THE UNITED STATES. Washington, D.C.: Government Printing Office, 1878-- .

> For a century, the abstract constitutes a standard summary of statistics covering various aspects of the United States, including immigration and deportation. Reflects immigration of Romanians and other ethnics by place of birth. Also indicates geographical distribution, sex, age, literacy level of the immigrants. Starting in 1921, shows annual quotas for Romania and other countries, and starting in 1953, incorporates statistics on persons admitted as refugees.

C-88 U.S. Department of Labor. ANNUAL REPORT OF THE COMMISSIONER OF IMMIGRATION. Washington, D.C.: Government Printing Office, 1899-- .

> Important source of information regarding Romanian immigration to America. Reflects entries from and departures to Romania. Starting in 1908, records indicate land of origin, sex, age, literacy, marital status, and even the amounts of money brought by immigrants. Also, relatives living in America, profession or occupation, destination, and other aspects. The statistics furnished by the Immigration Commissioner do not coincide with other sources.

Monographs

C-89 Carpenter, Niles, ed. IMMIGRANTS AND THEIR CHILDREN: 1920:

A STUDY BASED ON CENSUS STATISTICS RELATIVE TO THE FOREIGN BORN AND THE NATIVE WHITE OF FOREIGN OR MIXED PARENTAGE. Washington, D.C.: Government Printing Office, 1927. xvi, 431 p. Index.

Discusses several aspects of immigration--social, economic, occupation, geographical distribution, first and second generations, language, and so forth--regarding various ethnic groups including the Romanians. Of interest to researchers.

C-90 Hutchinson, Edward Prince, ed. IMMIGRANTS AND THEIR CHILDREN, 1850-1950. Census Monograph Series, vol. 3. New York: Wiley, 1956. 391 p. Index.

A study prepared for the Social Science Research Council in cooperation with the U.S. Department of Commerce, Bureau of the Census. Examines several facets of Romanian immigration to America--economic, social, literacy, professions and occupations, language, and so forth--in connection with and comparison to other immigrant groups. Based on the 1950 U.S. Census data. Bibliography.

Periodical Literature

C-91 "How Many Are We? Where Do We Live." AMERICAN ROMANIAN REVIEW 2 (May-June 1978): 15-17.

A critical examination of official statistical data on Romanians in America. Author believes that presently there are about 57,000-62,000 Romanian Americans, mainly living in Ohio, New York, Illinois, Michigan, Indiana, California, and New Jersey. According to the 1970 U.S. Census data, 216,000 Romanian Americans were recorded at that date. See also entries 1-45 to 1-68.

D. HISTORY AND RELATED AREA STUDIES

AMERICA—LAND OF ADOPTION

Monograph

D-1   Selisteanul, Ilie Martin. ISTORIA AMERICII [The history of America].
        2 vols. Cleveland: Union of Romanian Societies of America, 1903.
        Pap.

> The history of America--from the very beginnings to the
> twentieth century--presented in a straightforward manner from a
> patriotic viewpoint. Destined for newly arrived Romanian
> immigrants. The author was one of the early founders of the
> Romanian American benevolent societies. Of interest to re-
> searchers.

Periodical Literature

D-2   Barbul, George. "Istoria Statelor Unite" [The history of the United
        States." CALENDARUL RUMANUL (1909): 37-67.

> Condensed history of the United States, written in a popular
> style for newly arrived Romanian immigrants to America.

Colonial Period

PERIODICAL LITERATURE

D-3   Dvoichenko-Markov, Demetrius. "A Rumanian Priest in Colonial America."
        AMERICAN SLAVIC AND EAST EUROPEAN REVIEW 15 (October 1955):
        383-89.

> A detailed study devoted to Samuel Damian, a Romanian Ortho-
> dox priest from Transylvania, who came to America in 1748
> and marked the first Romanian presence on American soil.
> Spent several years in America, and favorably impressed
> Benjamin Franklin with electrical experiments.

Civil War

MONOGRAPHS

D-4   Belknap, Gen. William Worth. HISTORY OF THE FIFTEENTH REGI-
MENT, IOWA VETERAN VOLUNTEER INFANTRY: FROM OCTOBER
1861 TO AUGUST 1865. Keokuk, Iowa: R.B. Ogden and Son, 1867.
644 p. Index.

    A detailed history of the regiment led by George Pomutz, a
Romanian American later elevated to the rank of U.S. general,
who bravely defended the Union's cause. The book is based
on records prepared and examined by George Pomutz, whose
short biography, picture, and farewell address to the regiment
are included (pp. 38-39, 175, 186-89, 209-14, 507-9).

D-5   U. S. Department of War. A COMPILATION OF THE WAR OF THE
REBELLION OFFICIAL RECORDS OF THE UNION AND CONFEDERATE
ARMIES. 49 vols. Washington, D.C.: Government Printing Office,
1886. Index.

    Numerous records of this multivolume set reflect the bravery
displayed by George Pomutz as General Belknap's subordinate
during the Civil War, Pomutz's military actions in the capacity
of commander of the Fifteenth Iowa Regiment, orders received
from superiors, reports, and other relevant documents.

PERIODICAL LITERATURE

D-6   Borza, John, Jr. "Two Romanians in the Civil War." NEW PIONEER
1 (February 1943): 5-7.

    Short biographical sketches devoted to Captain Nicholas Dunca
and General George Pomutz, two Romanian Americans who
distinguished themselves during the Civil War defending the
Union's cause. Based on historical documents, and accompanied by pictures.

D-7   "A Commemoration of Two Civil War Heroes: General George Pomutz
and Captain Nicholas Dunca." AMERICA, June 4, 1932, pp. 1-2.

    Short presentation of the lives and deeds of two Romanian
American heroes.

D-8   Fillman, George. "Captain Nicolai Dunca: 1835-1862." CALEN-
DARUL SOLIA (1976): 140-44.

    A very well documented account of Dunca's life and historical
conditions preceding his immigration to America, participation
in the Civil War fighting on the Union's side under the orders

of General John C. Fremont, and death during the battle of
Key Cross, Virginia. The article is in English. Short bibliography and a picture of Dunca's grave.

D-9   _____. "General George Pomutz: 1818-1882." CALENDARUL
SOLIA (1976): 137-39.

Well-documented article on George Pomutz, his bravery during
the Civil War, and elevation to the rank of general. The
article is in English. Brief bibliography and a picture of
George Pomutz.

D-10   "George Pomutz." IOWA JOURNAL OF HISTORY AND POLITICS 11
(Fall 1913): 503-4.

Short biography of George Pomutz, his activities before the
Civil War, military accomplishments during the war, as well
as postwar activities in the capacity of U.S. consul general
in St. Petersburg, Russia.

Spanish-American War

PERIODICAL LITERATURE

D-11   Fillman, George. "Constantin Todoresco: 1863-1898." CALENDARUL
SOLIA (1977): 157-60.

An article devoted to an early Romanian American who gave
his life during the Spanish American while serving on the
U.S.S. MAINE, and was buried in Arlington Cemetery.
Written in English. Brief bibliography.

World War I

PERIODICAL LITERATURE AND PAMPHLETS

D-12   "Lista de Onoare a Comparatorilor de Liberty Bonduri" [The list of
honor of liberty bonds buyers]. AMERICA, January 27, 1919, p. 1.

A list of Romanian American organizations and their contributions to America's financial war efforts. At the beginning of
1919 the Romanian American organizations acquired bonds for
a total of $1,246,500.

D-13   Parvu, Ilie I. VOLUNTARII ROMANI DIN AMERICA [The Romanian
volunteers in America]. Sibiu, Romania: Kraft and Drotleff, 1937.
32 p. Pap.

A short but very interesting study on the Romanian American volunteers during the years 1917-18, and their contributions within the American Expeditionary Force in Europe on the French front. Official documents and a list of volunteers are appended.

D-14   "Romanian Volunteers in the American Army." AMERICAN ROMANIAN REVIEW 2 (March-April 1978): 6-9.

Short background information on Romanian immigrants who enrolled in the American and Canadian armies as volunteers during World War I. The Romanians of Youngstown, Ohio, were the first volunteers, and their leader was Sergeant Rudi Nan.

D-15   "Un Brav Ostean Roman American" [A brave Romanian American soldier]. AMERICA, June 13, 1935, pp. 1-2.

Biographical sketch of Corporal Dumitru Comsa who fought in France as a member of the American Expeditionary Force, together with other Romanian American volunteers, during World War I.

World War II

PERIODICAL LITERATURE

D-16   "In Memoriam." NEW PIONEER 1 (July-September 1943): 27; 2 (January 1944): 17-18; (February 1944): 10; 3 (January 1945): 22-29; (February 1945): 15-20; (March 1945): 5-7; (April 1945): 25-27; 4 (January 1946): 7.

Lists of Romanian Americans who gave their lives on various battle fronts while serving in the U.S. armed forces.

D-17   "Lieutenant Alex Vraciu, the Indestructible." NEW PIONEER 3 (February 1944): 27.

Short article devoted to a brave Romanian American pilot and his daring missions on the Pacific front.

D-18   "Lieut. Vraciu, Navy Top Ace Is of Romanian Descent." NEW PIONEER 2 (October 1944): 10-11.

Short biography of Alex Vraciu, born in East Chicago, Indiana, who downed nineteen Japanese planes. Picture.

D-19   "Military News." NEW PIONEER 2 (October 1944): 18-20.

Romanian Americans taking part in the military actions of the Allied Forces on June 6, 1944, in Normandie, France.

D-20 "Our Heroes." NEW PIONEER 1 (November 1942): 6-9; 2 (February 1943): 16-25; (April 1943): 20-25; (July-September 1943): 35-47; 3 (October 1944): 26-45.

> Lists of over five thousand Romanian men, accompanied by pictures, who served in the U.S. armed forces during World War II, and distinguished themselves on various fronts.

D-21 "Our Heroines." NEW PIONEER 2 (February 1943): 15; (April 1943): 89.

> Lists hundreds of Romanian American women who served in the U.S. armed forces or WAVE during World War II. Photographs included.

Post-World War II

PERIODICAL LITERATURE

D-22 "We Are Proud of Nicholas Daramus Jr." AMERICAN ROMANIAN REVIEW 1 (September 1977): 27.

> Short biographical sketch and picture of Nicholas Daramus, the first Romanian American to be elevated to the rank of full commander in the U.S. Navy.

HISTORY OF ORGANIZATIONS

Commemorative Issues

D-23 Fekett, Sofron S., ed. ISTORIA UNIUNII SI LIGII SOCIETATILOR ROMANESTI DIN AMERICA: 1906-1956 [The history of the Union and League of Romanian Societies of America: 1906-1956]. Cleveland: Union and League of Romanian Societies of America, 1956. 416 p. Pap.

> A commemorative issue highlighting the first fifty years of the oldest and largest Romanian American organization: its beginnings, history of various branches, problems, faction fights, consolidation, reorganization, press, achievements, attitudes toward the land of origin. Numerous and very good illustrations. Of special interest to historians.

D-24 ISTORICUL UNIUNII SI LIGII S.R.A. 1906-1931 [The history of the Union and League of Romanian Societies of America, 1906-1931]. Cleveland: America Press, 1932. 152 p.

> Commemorative issue celebrating the first twenty-five years of the most numerous Romanian American organization shortly

after it achieved unity within its ranks. Chronology of main events and presentation of seventy-five branches are included.

D-25 Lucaci, Peter, ed. CALENDARUL ZIARULUI AMERICA: 1976 [The almanac of the newspaper America: 1976]. Cleveland: Union and League of the Romanian Societies of America, 1976. 272 p.

This bicentennial and bilingual issue is devoted to Romanian contributions to AMERICA. It sheds light on the history of the Union and League of Romanian Societies and its activities, on Romanian American religious bodies--Baptist, Catholic (Eastern Rite), and Orthodox--and on the Iuliu Maniu Foundation. Also, includes a directory of organizations and relevant illustrations.

D-26 _____. "Iuliu Maniu, 1873-1952." CALENDARUL AMERICA (1962): 45-228.

Several articles commemorating Iuliu Maniu, prominent Romanian politician from Transylvania, fighter for freedom and democracy, strongly supported by Romanian Americans who immigrated from Transylvania. Numerous illustrations. Maniu's name had been adopted by the American Romanian Relief Foundation in New York City.

D-27 Metes, Rozeta M. THE IULIU MANIU AMERICAN-ROMANIAN RELIEF FOUNDATION. A QUARTER CENTURY OF ACTIVITY: 1951-1976. New York: Iuliu Maniu Foundation, 1976. 21 p. Pap.

After a short history of the main periods of Romanian immigration to America, the study focuses on the foundation's main activities and achievements: assistance to Romanian refugees and exiles, grants to deserving students, cultural programs, art collection, and library.

Periodical Literature

D-28 Butiu, Constantin. "Romanii din Canada Vor sa Intre in Uniunea si Liga" [The Romanians of Canada want to join the Union and League]. ROMANUL, May 19, 1929, p. 2.

Short article on Romanian Canadians who expressed their desire to join the Union and League of Romanian Societies of America.

D-29 Teodorescu, Paul G. "Historic Foundation of Romanian Studies Association of America." AMERICA, June 15, 1974, p. 10.

Short background information on the establishment, scope, and future plans of the association, which came into existence in

1973, and reunites several American college and university pro-
fessors interested in Romanian language and literature. See
also entries I-30 to I-44a.

ROMANIA—LAND OF ORIGIN

Monograph

D-30 Barlea, Octavian. ROMANIA SI ROMANII--ROMANIA AND THE RO-
MANIANS. Tr. by George Muresan. Los Angeles: American Romanian
Academy, 1977. 421 p.

Bilingual book dealing with Romania's people, land, history,
language, religion, literature, economic life, and other aspects. Good for Romanian American youth and others interested in Romanian heritage. The author and the translator are
noted Romanian Catholic leaders in America.

D-31 Stoica, Vasile. THE ROMANIANS AND THEIR LAND. 4 vols. Pittsburgh: Pittsburgh Printing Co., New York: G.H. Doran Co., 1919.
Pap.

A short history of the Romanian people and the regions of
Romania from ancient to modern times, advocating Romania's
rights to extend its sovereignity over Transylvania, Bucovina,
and Bessarabia, three regions under foreign domination before
the conclusion of World War I. The author was a prominent
Romanian American leader and his views reflected the feelings
of early Romanian immigrants to America and Canada, who came
mainly from the above regions.

D-32 Trifa, Bishop Valerian. ROMANIA: THE LAND, THE HISTORY, THE
PEOPLE. Pref. by Ileana, Princess of Romania. Tr. by Rev. Fr. Vasile
Hategan. Photos. by Alexandre Th. Petit. Jackson, Mich.: Romanian
Orthodox Episcopate of America, 1961. Unpaged.

Mostly a collection of views from Romania. Good companion
to the monographs cited above. Of interest to Romanian heritage students. The author is the head of the Romanian Orthodox Episcopate of America.

Transylvania

MONOGRAPH

D-33 Stoica, Vasile. SUFERINTELE DIN ARDEAL [The sufferings in Ardeal].
Chicago: Editura Tribunei, 1917. 386 p.

A history of the Romanians in Transylvania (also called Ardeal) and their oppression by the Hungarian rulers from 1526 to 1914. Includes a chronology of main events. Justified the demand that Transylvania be part of Romania, a demand made by Romanian Americans, since many immigrants came from this region and personally experienced the Hungarian oppression.

Vlad the Impaler—Dracula

MONOGRAPH

D-34 Florescu, Radu, and McNally, Raymond T. DRACULA: A BIOGRAPHY OF VLAD THE IMPALER, 1431-1476. New York: Hawthorn Books, 1973. 239 p. Index.

A biography of Dracula, whose real name was Vlad the Impaler, to dispel all myths that have arisen during the five centuries since his death. The study of the fifteenth-century Wallachian prince is based on several years of research. Extensive bibliography.

D-35 McNally, Raymond T., and Florescu, Radu. IN SEARCH OF DRACULA: A TRUE HISTORY OF DRACULA AND VAMPIRE LEGENDS. Westport, Conn.: Greenwich Press, 1972. 223 p. Index.

A miniature encyclopedic and pictorial essay on the elements contributing to the Dracula story originating from Bram Stoker's 1897 novel. It includes a short sketch of Dracula's life and the ancient and vampire traditions in Translyvania. It also covers the Gothic genre, Stoker's novel, and a brief history of Dracula films.

PERIODICAL LITERATURE

D-36 Andreescu, Stefan. "Vlad the Impaler--Dracula." CALENDARUL ZIARULUI AMERICA (1977): 177-93.

A well-documented article in English, aimed at establishing the historical truth about Dracula. He is presented as an illustrious political and military personality of his time.

D-37 Barsan, Vasile C. "Dracula: A Warped Image of Escapism and Insanity." ROMANIAN SOURCES 1 (1975): 44-54.

The main thesis of this extensive article is that Dracula never existed in Romanian folklore and history. The author, a Romanian American professor at Mankato State College, offers several arguments against the findings and interpretations made by Radu Florescu and Raymond T. McNally in their two books on Dracula (see entries D-34 and D-35).

E. PURE AND APPLIED SCIENCES

BIOLOGICAL SCIENCES

Reference Works

E-1   Jaques Cattell Press, ed. AMERICAN MEN AND WOMEN OF SCIENCE.
13th ed. Vol. 5. New York: R.R. Bowker Co., 1976. Index.

> Includes a short biographical sketch of Dr. George Emil Palade,
> world-renowned Romanian American scientist. Focuses on his
> activities and achievements in the United States, including the
> Nobel Prize.

E-2   Marquis Who's Who, ed. WHO'S WHO IN AMERICA: 1978–79. 40th
ed. 2 vols. Chicago: 1978.

> The second volume of this standard reference biographical work
> has an entry for Dr. George Emil Palade--personal data, pro-
> fessional activities, and publications (p. 2484).

E-3   Moritz, Charles, ed. CURRENT BIOGRAPHY YEARBOOK: 1967. New
York: H.W. Wilson Co., 1967. 513 p. Index.

> Extensive biographical sketch (pp. 324–26) of Dr. George Emil
> Palade, whose studies led to the discovery of ribosomes and
> the characterization of cell fractions. Lists all his achievements
> since Palade settled in America, as well as published works and
> scientific awards. Photograph included.

Periodical Literature

E-4   "Dr. George Emil Palade." NEW YORK POST, November 17, 1966,
p. 47.

> Short presentation of Palade's scientific work. Accompanied by
> picture.

E-5 _____. NEW YORK TIMES, December 15, 1959, p. 28.

> Palade offers evidence that particles are transported from blood
> to body tissues through capillary walls. Opens new vistas in
> medical research.

E-6 _____. NEW YORK TIMES, November 16, 1966, p. 56.

> Report on new biological discoveries and contributions made
> by Palade. Picture.

E-7 "Three Noble Laureats in Medicine." NEW YORK TIMES, October 11,
1974, p. 22.

> Short biography and picture of George Emil Palade, one of the
> three Nobel Prize winners in 1974. Palade won the prize for
> his contributions to the discovery of the cell factory secrets.
> The article brings up to date Palade's professional and scientific
> work, as well as his family life.

MATHEMATICS

Reference Works

E-8 Marquis Who's Who, ed. WHO'S WHO IN AMERICA: 1978-79. 40th
ed. 2 vols. Chicago: 1977.

> The second volume has an entry (p. 3,219) for Radu Theodorescu,
> mathematician and university professor at Laval University of
> Quebec, Canada. Biographical data, professional activities,
> writings, and membership.

Dictionaries

E-9 Gould, S.H., and Orbreanu, P.E., eds. ROMANIAN-ENGLISH DIC-
TIONARY AND GRAMMAR FOR MATHEMATICAL SCIENCES. Provi-
dence, R.I.: American Mathematical Society, 1967. 51 p. Pap.

> Short but very useful dictionary for students and scholars, ac-
> companied by an outline of the Romanian grammar. Obreanu is
> a professor of mathematics in Canada.

PHYSICS

Monograph

E-10 Bothezat, George De. BACK TO NEWTON, A CHALLENGE TO EIN-
STEIN'S THEORY OF RELATIVITY. New York: G.E. Stechart and Co.,
1936. vii, 152 p.

A study on space, time, and motion. Criticizes Einstein's theory of relativity, considering it harmful to human progress. The author was a Romanian aerodynamics engineer who came to America after World War I, and believed that Einstein's main contribution had been in the field of statistical mechanics.

PSYCHOLOGY AND PSYCHIATRY

Biographical Reference

E-11   Jaques Cattell Press, ed. BIOGRAPHICAL DIRECTORY OF THE FELLOWS AND MEMBERS OF THE AMERICAN PSYCHIATRIC ASSOCIATION. New York: Xerox Education Companies, 1977. 1,573 p.

This well-known compilation includes a biographical entry (p. 66) for Valer Barbu, a Romanian American psychiatrist, disciple of Karen Horney. Main biographical data, professional activities, writings, membership.

Monographs

E-12   Barbu, Valer. METODA IN PSIHIATRIE SI ROLUL PSIHIATRIEI IN MEDICINA [The psychiatric method and its role in medicine]. Arad, Romania: Concordia Institut de Arte Grafice si Editura, 1935. 82 p. Pap.

A brochure intending to share with Romanian readers the author's experience at Henry Phipps Clinic at Johns Hopkins University and Payne Whitney Clinic at Cornell University. The brochure was written in New York City, but published in Romania to acquaint Romanian specialists with American psychiatric methods.

E-13   Horney, Karen, ed. ARE YOU CONSIDERING PSYCHOANALYSIS? New York: W.W. Norton and Co., 1946. 260 p. Index.

The chapter "What Schools of Psychoanalysis Are They?" (pp. 37-59, dealing with Sigmund Freud, Alfred Adler, Otto Rank, Carl G. Jung, and Karen Horney) was written by Valer Barbu, a Romanian American psychiatrist. Barbu supported Karen Horney's theoretical concepts of treating neurosis, that one should seek the origin of the disease in the individual character rather than in sexual factors.

ENGINEERING

Monographs

E-14   Gardescu, Ionel. "The Occurence on Behavior of Natural Gas in an

Oil Reservoir." Ph.D. dissertation, University of California, Berkeley, 1931. 128 p.

The first doctoral dissertation by a Romanian American in the field of petroleum engineering.

E-15 Vasiliu, John W. "An Investigation of the Influence of Heat Capacity Lag on the Flow Parameters in an Expansion through Short Mach Number Two Nozzle." Ph.D. dissertation, Columbia University, 1951. 173 p.

A doctoral thesis on gas flow and heat transmission in the field of electrical engineering.

Periodical Literature

E-16 Barbulescu, Constantin D. "Automatic Control of Aircraft." ELECTRICAL ENGINEERING 60 (March 1941): 122-26; ELECTRIC NEWS AND ENGINEERING 50 (April 1, 1941): 34-37.

Well-documented article devoted to methods of controlling aircrafts through electromagnetic radiations in any kind of weather. The author was a noted Romanian American aeronautical engineer.

E-17 Papana, Alex. "I Learned about Flying from That." FLYING 37 (November 1945): 48.

A noted Romanian American test pilot describes the beginnings of his career. Accompanied by picture.

E-18 _____. "What You Should Know about Compressibility." FLYING 38 (April 1946): 66-67.

A professional article written by Papana shortly before his death, when he worked as a test pilot for Northrop Aircraft, California. Picture.

D-19 "Primul Aviator Roman in America" [The first Romanian pilot in America]. AMERICA, July 13, 1911, p. 1.

Short background information on Alexander Taflan, a Romanian American pilot of Sharon, Pennsylvania, who built a new type of American airplane.

MEDICAL SCIENCES

Biographical Reference

E-20 Marquis Who's Who, ed. WHO'S WHO IN THE EAST: 1977-78. 16th ed. Chicago: 1977. 875 p.

In this standard reference work there is an entry (p. 762) for Constantin V. Teodoru, prominent Romanian American rheumatologist and professor at New York University. Biographical data, professional activities, and membership.

Periodical Literature

E-21   "Dr. Traian Leucutia." AMERICAN ROMANIAN REVIEW 1 (October-November 1977): 22.

Biographical sketch of a distinguished Romanian American radiologist, who started his career in 1921, pioneered against electrical and radiation hazards of X-rays, and served as editor of the AMERICAN JOURNAL OF ROENTGENOLOGY, RADIUM THERAPY AND NUCLEAR MEDICINE.

E-22   "Dr. Traian Leucutia: An Outstanding Romanian Immigrant in America." CALENDARUL SOLIA (1978): 121-24.

Another biographical sketch of Leucutia, accompanied by picture and detailed listing of academic achievements, including postgraduate work, teaching positions, membership in professional societies, honorary titles.

Nursing

MONOGRAPH

E-23   Wright, Helen, and Rapaport, Samuel eds. GREAT ADVENTURES IN NURSING. New York: Harper and Row, 1961. 288 p. Index.

Collective biography of noted women who devoted their lives to the sick, including Princess Ileana. She was a former member of the Romanian royal family, presently a Romanian Orthodox nun residing in Pennyslvania.

HOME ECONOMICS: COOKING

Monographs—General

E-24   Donovan, Maria Kozlik. THE BLUE DANUBE COOKBOOK. Garden City, N.Y.: Doubleday & Co., 1967. 258 p. Index.

Romanian cooking is profusely represented by several dozen good recipes ranging from one-course meals, garnishes, salads, and soups, to meats, fish, poultry, and game, with special attention to Transylvanian food. The titles of dishes are in

English with Romanian subtitles, as known by Romanian American housewives.

E-25   Howe, Robin. BALKAN COOKING. New York: London House and Maxwell, 1965. 272 p. Index.

A very rich assortment of Romanian recipes (hors d'oeuvres, salads, egg varieties, fish, meats, soups, sauces, etc.) from various regions. Useful for student assignments, but of special interest to chefs and those willing to specialize in Romanian gastronomy. English names of dishes with Romanian subtitles.

E-26   London, Anne. THE AMERICAN-INTERNATIONAL ENCYCLOPEDIC COOKBOOK. New York: Thomas Y. Crowell, 1972. 1,016 p. Index.

Includes recipes for four Romanian dishes: eggplant caviar, hamburger rolls, corn mush meal, pancakes. Good for quick reference.

E-27   Olesky, Walter. THE OLD COUNTRY COOKBOOK. Chicago: Nelson-Hall, 1974. 402 p. Index.

The chapter devoted to Romanian food has only one dozen Romanian recipes, but all are popular and easy to prepare. English names of meals are accompanied by Romanian subtitles. A brief introduction on Romanian cooking precedes the recipes. Good for students.

E-28   Waldo, Myra. THE COMPLETE ROUND-THE-WORLD COOKBOOK. Garden City, N.Y.: Doubleday & Co., 1973. 258 p. Index.

Popular cookbook covering several ethnic groups. Short introduction on Romanian meals and their main features, with ten recipes for typical Romanian dishes: caviar Romanian style, sour soup, baked fish with vegetables, beans--peasant style, pear compote, and others. Good for quick reference and student assignments. Romanian subtitles accompany English titles of dishes.

Monographs—Special

E-29   Polvay, Marina. THE DRACULA COOKBOOK. New York: Chelsea House, 1978. 186 p. Index.

Two hundred recipes with a Dracula motif, including the dinners he served his victims, food to ward off vampires, aphrodisiacs, and so forth. But all are authentic regional recipes from Transylvania. Accompanied by illustrations.

E-30   Stan, Anisoara. THE ROMANIAN COOK BOOK. Illus. by John Teppich.

New York: Citadel Press, 1951. xiii, 229 p. Index.

Contains 450 recipes for a wide variety of Romanian dishes: eggplants, appetizers, hors d'oeuvres, soups, vegetables, mushrooms, fish, chicken, meats, stews, corn mush, dumplings, sauces, salads, desserts, and preserves. The only cookbook by a Romanian American woman, who used several Romanian American sources. Author's tips and suggestions facilitate cooking. Paperback edition in 1969.

Periodical Literature

E-31 "Cooking Notes." NEW PIONEER 1 (November 1942): 22; 2 (February 1943): 51; (July-September 1943): 54; 2 (January 1944): 35; (April 1944): 43; (July 1944): 40; (October 1944): 58; 3 (January 1945): 55; (April 1945): 52; (October 1945): 36; 4 (January 1946): 41; (April 1946): 35; (October 1946): 37; 5 (January-April 1947): 34; 6 (January-April 1948): 37; 6 (June-September 1948): 39.

Dozens of Romanian recipes--soups, meats, fish, salads, desserts, and so forth--collected from various Romanian American houses. The same recipes are used by Romanian Canadian housewives.

E-32 "Cooking Notes." AMERICAN ROMANIAN REVIEW 1 (September 1977): 41; (October 1977): 35; 2 (January 1978): 34; (February 1978): 32.

Additional recipes furnished by Romanian American housewives. Some recipes are accompanied by the English and Romanian names of herbs, vegetables, and spices frequently used in the preparation of Romanian dishes and pastries.

E-33 "Pofta Buna" [Bon appetit]. AMERICAN ROMANIAN REVIEW 2 (March-April 1978): 33; (May-June 1978): 28; (July-August 1978): 32.

Despite the Romanian title, the recipes are in English, and include, among others, suggestions for a Romanian Easter dinner.

Part 2

DIRECTORIES ADDENDUM

F. ROMANIAN-AMERICAN AND CANADIAN ORGANIZATIONS AND INSTITUTIONS

This section lists 148 Romanian American and Romanian Canadian national organizations and institutions, both active and retrospective, as well as local organizations affiliated with the Union and League of Romanian Societies of America (U.L.R.S.A.)

For organizations and institutions of national importance, each entry provides the following information: name, address, year of establishment, purpose, and other relevant data (when available), such as membership, publications, and affiliation with other organizations.

For local organizations, besides names and addresses, the year of establishment (or merger) is mentioned whenever known. There are also translations of Romanian names, and annotations regarding various Romanian personalities.

Addresses of Romanian American and Canadian auxiliary and local organizations are often subject to changes. Usually, the addresses are of the presiding officers or secretaries, and as soon as new officers are elected, the addresses are changed. Therefore, the latest and updated list of addresses are kept by national organizations with permanent headquarters.

NATIONAL ASSOCIATIONS, ORGANIZATIONS, AND INSTITUTIONS

F-1   AMERICAN ROMANIAN ACADEMY OF ARTS AND SCIENCES. 265 Lee Street, Oakland, Calif. 94610.

> Established in 1975. Aim: Promotion of Romanian culture in the United States, Canada, and other countries outside Romania. Members are elected for life on the basis of their works (human sciences, art, science, religion). There are also associates and correspondents residing outside the United States.

F-2   AMERICAN ROMANIAN HERITAGE FOUNDATION. 17313 Puritas Avenue, Cleveland, Ohio 44135.

Established in 1975. Aim: Preservation of Romanian heritage in the United States and Canada, popularization of Romanian American and Canadian achievements and contributions. Publishes AMERICAN ROMANIAN REVIEW (see entry H-3).

F-3   AMERICAN ROMANIAN ORTHODOX YOUTH (A.R.O.Y). 2522 Grey Tower Road, R.F.D. No. 7, Jackson, Mich. 49201.

Established in 1952. Aim: Preservation of Romanian Orthodox faith and popularization of Romanian ethnic values among Romanian American and Canadian youth. Membership: about 1,000. It is an auxiliary organization for youth of the Romanian Orthodox Episcopate of America. Besides religious training, it also offers various cultural activities.

F-4   ASSOCIATION OF ROMANIAN CATHOLICS OF AMERICA. 4309 Olcott Avenue, East Chicago, Ind. 46312.

Established in 1948. Aim: Preservation of Romanian Catholic (Eastern Rite) faith and popularization of Romanian ethnic values in the United States. Membership: about 4,000. Serves as a coordinating agency between eighteen Romanian Catholic parishes and their members, has a special youth department, publishes UNIREA (see entry H-21).

F-5   ASSOCIATION OF ROMANIAN ORTHODOX LADIES AUXILIARIES (A.R.O.L.A.). 14604 Ninety-seventh Avenue, Edmondon, Alberta.

Established in 1972. Aim: To assist Romanian Orthodox parishes in religious, cultural, social, and charitable activities. It is an auxiliary organization of the Romanian Orthodox Missionary Diocese of America.

F-6   ASSOCIATION OF ROMANIAN ORTHODOX LADIES AUXILIARIES OF NORTH AMERICA (A.R.F.O.R.A.). 766 Squirrel Hill Court, Youngstown, Ohio 44512.

Established in 1938. Aim: To assist the Romanian Orthodox parishes in religious, cultural, social, ethnic, and charitable activities. It is an auxiliary organization of the Romanian Orthodox Episcopate of America.

F-7   IULIU MANIU AMERICAN ROMANIAN RELIEF FOUNDATION. 55 West Forty-second Street, New York, N.Y. 10036.

Established in 1952. Aim: Preservation of Romanian ethnic values in America, assistance to Romanian refugees and exiles, grants for deserving students. Membership: about 300. Involved in various cultural, social, and publishing activities.

F-8   THE ORTHODOX BROTHERHOOD. 11341 Woodward Avenue, Detroit, Mich. 48202.

> Established in 1952. Aim: Preservation of Romanian Orthodox faith in America and Canada, and assistance to Romanian Orthodox parishes in religious, social, and other activities. It is an auxiliary organization of the Roman Orthodox Episcopate of America.

F-9   ROMANIAN AMERICAN HERITAGE CENTER. 2522 Grey Tower Road, Jackson, Mich. 49201.

> Established in 1975. Aim: Development of a center for study and research of Romanian heritage in America and Canada. Functions under the auspices of the Romanian Orthodox Episcopate of America.

F-10   ROMANIAN BAPTIST ASSOCIATION OF THE UNITED STATES AND CANADA. c/o Rev. Danila Pascu, 9410 Clifton Boulevard, Cleveland, Ohio 44102

> Established in 1916. Aim: Preservation of Romanian Baptist faith in America and Canada. Serves as a coordinating agency for Romanian Baptist churches and their members. Publishes LUMINATORUL (see entry H-13). Associated with the American Baptist Churches in the U.S.A., member of the North American Baptist Fellowship.

F-11   ROMANIAN BAPTIST YOUTH FELLOWSHIP. 1414 North Lockwood Avenue, Chicago, Ill. 60651.

> Established in 1929. Aim: Coordination of missionary activities among Romanian American youth, and promotion of unity within the Romanian Baptist youth organizations.

F-12   ROMANIAN CHRISTIAN BAPTIST INSTITUTE. 348 Cole Avenue and Sherman Street, Akron, Ohio 44301.

> Established in 1975. Aim: Promotion of Romanian Baptist faith in America, publication of appropriate literature; associated with the Southern Baptist Convention; publishes FARUL MANTUIRII and VIATA IN CHRISTOS (see entries H-12 and H-23).

F-13   ROMANIAN MISSIONARY SOCIETY. 801 South Ocean Drive, Hollywood, Fla. 33020.

> Established in 1968. Aim: Dissemination of Christian Baptist oriented literature and Gospel broadcasting, relief and medical aid to needy Romanian Baptists in America, Canada, and other countries.

F-14   ROMANIAN NATIONAL COUNCIL. P.O. Box A-111, Radio City
Station, New York, N.Y. 10019.

> Established in 1970. Aim: Development of closer ties between
> Romanian Americans and Romanians from other countries, and
> popularization of their achievements. Publishes ACTIUNEA
> ROMANEASCA (see entry H-1).

F-15   ROMANIAN ORTHODOX EPISCOPATE OF AMERICA. 2522 Grey Tower
Road, Jackson, Mich. 49201.

> Established in 1929, reorganized in 1951. Aim: Preservation
> of Romanian Orthodox faith in America and Canada, adminis-
> tration of parishes that fall under its jurisdiction, coordination
> of auxiliary organization activities. Membership: about
> 50,000. Lists thirty-four parishes in America, twelve parishes
> in Canada, and one parish in Argentina, South America (see
> Directory of Romanian Orthodox Parishes). It is an autocepha-
> lous religious body, canonically associated with the Orthodox
> Church in America. Publishes SOLIA (see entry H-20).

F-16   ROMANIAN ORTHODOX MISSIONARY ARCHDIOCESE IN AMERICA.
19959 Riopelle Street, Detroit, Mich. 48203.

> Established in 1929; reorganized in 1950. Aim: Preservation
> of Romanian Orthodox faith in America and Canada, adminis-
> tration of parishes that fall under its jurisdiction, coordination
> of auxiliary organization activities. Membership: about
> 15,000. Lists twelve parishes in America, nineteen parishes
> in Canada, and one parish in Venezuela (see Directory of
> Romanian Orthodox Parishes). It is under the canonical juris-
> diction of the Romanian Orthodox Patriarchate, with headquar-
> ters in Bucharest, Romania. Publishes CREDINTA (see entry H-8).

F-17   ROMANIAN ORTHODOX YOUTH IN AMERICA (R.O.Y.A). 194 East
Montana Street, Detroit, Mich. 48203.

> Established in 1972. Aim: Preservation of Romanian Orthodox
> faith, and popularization of Romanian ethnic values. It is an
> auxiliary organization of the Romanian Orthodox Missionary
> Diocese in America.

F-18   UNION AND LEAGUE OF ROMANIAN SOCIETIES OF AMERICA
(U.L.R.S.A.). 720 Williamson Building, 215 Euclid Avenue, Cleveland,
Ohio 44114.

> Established in 1906. Aim: Preservation of Romanian national
> culture, heritage, and identity in America and Canada, and
> provision of life insurance to members. Membership: about

5,000. Has fifty-six affiliated organizations in America, and six in Canada, (see Directory of Organization affiliated with U.L.R.S.A.). Resulted from the merger of the Union of Romanian American Societies and The League and Help in 1928, after several years of internecine fights. It is the largest, the oldest, and the most influential Romanian American and Canadian organization. Publishes AMERICA (see entry H-2).

ROMANIAN-AMERICAN VETERAN ORGANIZATIONS

F-19 CAPTAIN NICHOLAS DUNCA POST No. 314 OF THE AMERICAN LEGION. 1365 Andrews Avenue, Cleveland, Ohio 44107.

Chartered in 1940. Named after Captain Nicholas Dunca, a Romanian American who fought for the Union's cause during the Civil War and gave his life in 1862.

F-20 GENERAL GEORGE POMUTZ POST No. 343 OF THE AMERICAN LEGION. 17321 Lennane Street, Detroit, Mich. 48240.

Chartered in 1934. Named after George Pomutz, who distinguished himself in several battles during the Civil War, and was promoted to the rank of U.S. general, the highest rank ever reached by a Romanian American.

F-21 LEGION OF ROMANIAN AMERICAN VOLUNTEERS. Box 2557. Youngstown, Ohio 44507.

Chartered in 1927. Encompasses veterans of both world wars, the Korean War, and the Vietnam War.

ORGANIZATIONS AFFILIATED WITH THE UNION AND LEAGUE OF ROMANIAN SOCIETIES OF AMERICA

American Organizations

ARIZONA

F-22 RAZA SOARELUI (Ray of Sun). 5115 North Twelfth Street, Phoenix, Ariz. 85014.

Romanian name, but does not have special ethnic connotation.

CALIFORNIA

F-23 DOINA. 1051 Foothill Boulevard, LaCanada, Calif. 91011.

Doina is a genre of Romanian popular songs; organized in 1953.

Organizations and Institutions

F-24　UNIREA DELA VEST　(The Union of the West).　265 Lee Street, Oakland, Calif.　94610.

Allusion to the necessity of being united; organized in 1924.

F-25　VIITORUL ROMAN (The Romanian Future).　3315 Verdugo Road, Los Angeles, Calif.　90065.

Allusion to the preservation of ethnic heritage; organized in 1926.

CONNECTICUT

F-26　ANDREI MURESAN.　343 Grovers Avenue, Bridgeport, Conn.　06605.

Named after Andrei Muresan (1816-63), noted Romanian poet and patriot of Transylvania; organized in 1909.

FLORIDA

F-27　FLORIDA.　2223 Madison Street, Hollywood, Fla.　33020.

Florida state organization.

ILLINOIS

F-28　SPERANTA-EMIGRANTUL (Hope-Emigrant).　5541 West Hutchinson Street, Chicago, Ill.　60641.

Resulted from the merger of several organizations; initially organized in 1908.

INDIANA

F-29　CLUBUL NICOLAE IORGA (Nicolae Iorga Club).　P.O. Box 233, East Chicago, Ind.　46312.

Named after Nicholae Iorga (1871-1940), noted Romanian historian and scholar of international fame; organized in 1909.

F-30　FIII ROMANIEI (Romania's Sons).　1404 Glenwood Avenue, Fort Wayne, Ind.　46805.

Based on Romanian ethnic pride.

F-31　ROMANIAN LODGE 148.　808 East Sixty-first Street, Merrilville, Ind. 46410.

F-32　STEAUA ROMANA (The Romanian Star).　3237 West Sixteenth Street, Indianapolis, Ind.　46222.

Ethnic pride; organized in 1905.

F-33 STEFAN CEL MARE (Stephan the Great). 220 West King Street, Garrett, Ind. 46378.

> Named after Stephan the Great (1450-1504), noted Moldavian ruler and military man. Moldavia is a region in Eastern Romania; organized in 1911.

F-34 TRICOLORUL ROMAN (The Romanian Tricolor). 1451 Alabama Street, Hobart, Ind. 46342.

> The Romanian flag has three colors: red, yellow, and blue; organized in 1906.

F-35 UNIREA ROMANA (Romanian Unity). 4334 Todd Avenue, East Chicago, Ind. 46312.

> Allusion to the necessity of being united.

MICHIGAN

F-36 BUCOVINA. 18405 West Nine Mile Road, Southfield, Mich. 48075.

> Named after Bucovina, a region in the Northern part of Romania; organized in 1928.

F-37 DUNAREANA (The Danubian). 19451 Hilton Street, Southfield, Mich. 48075.

> Named after the river Danube which crosses the Southeastern part of Romania; organized in 1931.

F-38 GHEORGHE LAZAR. 1513 East State Fair, Detroit, Mich. 48203.

> Named after Gheorghe Lazar (1779-1823), noted Romanian scholar and founder of the Romanian education system; organized in 1924.

F-39 MARASESTI. P.O. Box 4034. Dearborn, Mich. 48203.

> Named after a locality in Romania where the Romanians defeated the Germans during World War I; organized in 1927.

F-40 MUNCITORUL ROMAN (The Romanian Worker). 60 Niagara Street, Pontiac, Mich. 48203.

> An organization composed of Romanian workers; organized in 1927.

F-41 ROMANIA. 73 West Arizona Street, Detroit, Mich. 48203.

> Patriotic, ethnic pride name.

F-42   TARA VECHE (Old Land).   1881 Larkmore Boulevard, Berkley, Mich. 48072.

Patriotic, ethnic pride name.

F-43   UNIREA ROMANILOR (United Romanians)   18405 West Nine Mile Road, Southfield, Mich.   48075.

Allusion to the necessity of being united; organized in 1924.

F-44   VIATA ROMANA-AMERICANA (Romanian-American Life).   29554 Chelmsford Street, Southfield, Mich.   48076.

MINNESOTA

F-45   ROMANII DIN MINNESOTA (The Romanians of Minnesota).   P.O. Box 414.   South St. Paul, Minn.   55076.

Organized in 1953 as a result of the merger between three local organizations.

MISSOURI

F-46   ANA VLAD.   5225 Lake Avenue, St. Joseph, Mo.   64504.

Named after Ana Vlad, noted Romanian woman activist.

NEBRASKA

H-47   FRANKLIN D. ROOSEVELT.   1805 Freeman Drive, Bellevue, Nebr.   68005.

Honoring an American president.

NEW JERSEY

F-48   SF. MARIA ROMANIAN SOCIETY AND CLUB.   300 Norman Avenue, Roebling, N.J.   85014.

Named after St. Mary.

F-49   VOLUNTARII ROMANIEI (Romania's Volunteers).   Second Street, R.D. Hedding, Bordentown, N.J.   08505.

Patriotic, ethnic pride; organized in 1917.

NEW YORK

F-50   AVRAM IANCU.   50 West 89th Street, New York, N.Y.   10024.

Named after Avram Iancu (1824-72), noted Romanian patriot and leader of the 1848 revolution in Transylvania; organized in 1909.

F-51   SF. GEORGHE SI ADEVARUL (St. Gheorghe and the Truth).   7 Sand-
rock Road, Buffalo, N.Y.   19207.

>Resulted from the merger of two societies: St. George and
>Truth.

OHIO

F-52   APOLZANA.   720 Taylor Street, Hubbrad,   Ohio   44425.

>Named after a locality of Transylvania, Romanian region;
>organized in 1914.

F-53   CUZA VODA-TARA OLTULUI (Leader Cuza- Land of Olt).   3520 7th
Street, S.W., Canton, Ohio   44710.

>Resulted from the merger of two societies.   Alexandru Ion
>Cuza was the first Romanian ruler (1859-66) who united two
>Romanian provinces, Moldavia and Wallachia, into a national
>state.   Oltenia is a part of Wallachia; organized in 1912.

F-54   DACIA SI RENASTEREA ROMANA (Dacia and Romanian Revival).   P.O.
Box 25065.   Cincinnati, Ohio   45225.

>Resulted from the merger of two societies: Dacia, named after
>the ancient name of present-day Romania, and Romanian Re-
>vival; organized in 1906.

F-55   DACIA TRAIANA (Trajan's Dacia).   477 Heath, R.D. 5, Newark,Ohio
43055.

>Named after Dacia after it was occupied by Roman Emperor
>Trajan (191-6) A.D. and renamed Romania; organized in 1906.

F-56   DESTEPTAREA NEAMULUI SI BIRUINTA (The Awakening of the People
and Victory).   1717 Youngstown Road, Warren, Ohio   44483.

>Resulted from the merger of two societies; both with patriotic
>names; organized in 1912.

F-57   FRATIA SI SEMANATORUL (Brotherhood and the Sower).   30 Bright
Avenue, Youngstown, Ohio   44405.

>Resulted from the merger of two societies.

F-58   FRATII ROMANI (Romanian Brothers).   135 South Chestnut Street, Niles,
Ohio   44446.

>Patriotic, ethnic pride; organized in 1908.

F-59   FURNICA (The Ant). 5859 Murnen Road, Toledo, Ohio   43623.

The ant symbolizes hard work.

F-60   IZVORUL (The Spring). 4933 Sampson Drive, Youngstown, Ohio   44505.

Alluding to the original source of ethnicity; organized in 1919.

F-61   LEUL (The Lion). 387 South Ellsworth, Salem, Ohio   44460.

Symbolizes courage; organized in 1906.

F-62   PATRIA ROMANA SI BIHOREANA (The Romanian Fatherland and Biho-reana). 2217 East Twenty-eighth Street, Lorain, Ohio   44055.

Resulted from the merger of two societies: one honoring the original land of immigrants, the second a county in Transylvania; organized in 1907.

F-63   ROMANIA LIBERA A NEAMULUI ROMANESC (Free Romania of the Romanian People). 1577 Berendo Avenue, Akron, Ohio   44313.

Patriotic, ethnic pride; organized in 1912.

F-64   TRAIAN SI IULIU MANIU (Trajan and Iuliu Maniu). 2312 Coventry Boulevard, N.E., Canton, Ohio   44705.

Resulted from the merger of two societies; one named after Roman Emperor Trajan, the second after Iuliu Maniu (1873–1952), prominent Romanian politician and fighter for democracy; organized in 1909.

F-65   UNIREA ROMANA TRANSILVANEANA (Transylvanian Romanian Unity). 20 South Seneca Street, Alliance, Ohio   44601.

Named after Transylvania, Romanian region; organized in 1903.

F-66   UNIREA SI PLUGARUL (Unity and the Ploughman). 559 Garfield Street, Youngstown, Ohio   44503.

Resulted from the merger of two societies; organized in 1903.

F-67   U.S.R. CARPATINA (The Carpathian Union). 21250 Seabury Avenue, Cleveland, Ohio   44126.

Named after the Carpathian Mountains, which embrace a part of Romania; the oldest Romanian American society; organized in 1902.

PENNSYLVANIA

F-68   ADEVARUL-AURORA SI FIII ROMANIEI (Truth, Dawn, Sons of Romania).

1312 East Woodland Street, Allentown, Pa. 18103.

Resulted from the merger of three organizations, the earliest founded in 1916.

F-69   ALBINA (The Bee). 1120 Cunningham Avenue, New Castle, Pa. 16101.

The bee symbolizes hard work; organized in 1906.

F-70   CAROL I. R.D. 2, Beaver Falls, Pa. 15010.

Named after Carol I (1881-1914), the first Romanian monarch.

F-71   LUMINA SI PROGRESUL (Light and Progress). P.O. Box 228, Aliquippa, Pa. 15001.

Resulted from the merger of two societies.

F-72   TRANSILVANIA LIBERA (Free Transylvania). 1247 Hall Avenue, Sharon, Pa. 16146.

Named after Transylvania, Romanian region.

F-73   ULPIA TRAIANA (Trajan's Ulpia). 1133 Pennsylvania Avenue, Erie, Pa. 16503.

Named after Roman Emperor Trajan, whose real name was Marcus Ulpius Traianus, the conqueror of ancient Dacia (101-6 A.D.); organized in 1906.

F-74   VULTURUL (The Eagle). 315 Seventh Street, West Homestead, Pa. 15120.

The eagle symbolizes courage and greatness; organized in 1903.

WASHINGTON, D.C.

F-75   DACIA FELIX. 1330 Massachusetts Avenue, Washington, D.C. 20005.

Ancient name of Romania, after Dacia was occupied by Emperor Trajan and transformed into a Roman colony.

WEST VIRGINIA

F-76   GLORIA ROMANA SI MIHAI VITEAZUL (Romanian Glory and Michael the Brave). 332 Lee Avenue, Weirton, W. Va. 26062.

Resulted from the merger of two societies; one with a patriotic, ethnic pride name, the second named after Michael the Brave (1593-1601), a noted Romanian ruler, who unified for the first time the provinces of Wallachia, Moldavia, and Transylvania; organized in 1912.

Organizations and Institutions

Canadian Organizations

F-77 CONSTANTIN BRANCOVEANU. 4920 Sir Geo. Simpson Street, Lachine, Quebec.

> Named after Constantin Brancoveanu (1688-1714), a Wallachian ruler; Wallachia is a Romanian region.

F-78 CULTURAL ASSOCIATION DACIA. 247 Rosethorn Avenue, Toronto, Ontario.

> Dacia was Romania's name before it was occupied by Emperor Trajan.

F-79 ENERGIA (Energy). 2070 West Fourteenth Avenue, Vancouver, British Columbia.

F-80 GRAIUL ROMANESC (The Romanian Speech). 1849 Chandler Road, Windsor, Ontario.

> Ethnic pride; organized in 1929.

F-81 ROMANIAN ASSOCIATION MIHAIL EMINESCU. 69 Irvin Street, Kitchener, Ontario.

> Named after Mihail Eminescu (1850-89), the greatest Romanian poet.

F-82 ROMANIAN CULTURAL ASSOCIATION. Box 4217, Station D, Hamilton, Ontario.

F-83 ROMANIAN CANADIAN ASSOCIATION OF ONTARIO. 1862 Eglinton Avenue West, Toronto, Ontario.

> Organized in 1973.

F-84 ROMANIAN CANADIAN CLUB OF MOOSE JAW. P.O. Box 275, Moose Jaw, Saskatchewan.

> Organized in 1974.

RETROSPECTIVE ROMANIAN-AMERICAN NATIONAL ORGANIZATIONS AND INSTITUTIONS

F-85 ASSOCIATION OF ROMANIAN ORTHODOX PRIESTS. Cleveland, Ohio.

> 1922-34. Aim: To protect the interests of Romanian Orthodox

priests who were ordained in America by a Russian bishop.

F-86 CULTURAL ASSOCIATION FOR AMERICANS OF ROMANIAN DESCENT. Cleveland, Ohio.

1942-48. Aim: preservation of Romanian heritage in America, popularization of Romanian contributions in America.

F-87 CULTURAL ASSOCIATION OF ROMANIAN WORKERS. Detroit, Mich.

1918-34. Aim: socialist propaganda, fight against the capitalist system.

F-88 DEMOCRATIC UNION OF FREE ROMANIANS. New York.

1948-52. Aim: promonarchist, restoration of King Michael (the last Romanian monarch who abdicated in 1947 under Communist pressure) to power.

F-89 FEDERATION OF ROMANIAN SOCIALIST WORKERS IN THE UNITED STATES. Detroit, Mich.

1914-36. Aim: Socialist propaganda, later openly pro-Communist, praising Soviet Union achievements; replaced by ROMANIAN AMERICAN MOVEMENT (see entry F-93).

F-90 FREE ROMANIA COMMITTEE. New York City.

1941-42. Aim: Anti-Fascist, fight for the restoration of King Carol II to the Romanian throne; the king had abdicated in 1940 under the pressure of Fascist forces.

F-91 LEAGUE OF FREE ROMANIANS. New York City.

1950-52. Aim: Anti-Communist, restoration of a democratic society in Romania.

F-92 ROMANIAN AMERICAN ALLIANCE FOR DEMOCRACY. Cleveland, Ohio.

1941-45. Aim: To support U.S. war efforts during World War II; opposed to the organizations supporting former Romanian monarchs.

F-93 ROMANIAN AMERICAN MOVEMENT. Detroit, Mich.

1936-67. Aim: Pro-Communist propaganda, branch of the former I.W.O. (International Workers Order).

F-94 ROMANIAN NATIONAL COMMITTEE. Washington, D.C.

1949-74. Aim: Anti-Communist, restoration of democracy in

Romania; supporting the last Romanian monarch--King Michael, presently in exile.

F-95   ROMANIAN NATIONAL LEAGUE OF AMERICA. Cleveland, Ohio.

1918. Aim: Opposed to Hungarian rule and oppression of Romanians in Transylvania.

F-96   ROMANIAN WELFARE. New York.

1948-74. Aim: Helping refugees and exiles from Romania and other Eastern European countries; accorded assistance--in money and food--to about seven thousand displaced persons.

F-97   UNION OF THE GREEK CATHOLIC SOCIETIES OF AMERICA. Cleveland, Ohio. 1924-48.

1924-48. Aim: Benevolent and cultural organization for Romanian American Catholics (Eastern Rite).

RETROSPECTIVE ORGANIZATIONS OF THE UNION AND LEAGUE OF ROMANIAN SOCIETIES OF AMERICA

Illinois

F-98   DR. EPAMINONDA LUCACIU. Aurora, Ill.

Named after Fr. Epaminonda Lucaciu (1877-1946), who established the first Romanian Catholic parish in America; organized in 1916.

F-99   EMIGANTUL (The Emigrant). Chicago, Ill.

Organized in 1909 by immigrants from Banat, Romanian region under Austro-Hungarian rule at that time; merged with SPERANTA in 1944 under the name SPERANTA-EMIGRANTUL.

F-100   FALNICUL ZARAND ROMAN (Remarkable Romanian Zarand). Clearing, Ill.

Named after a very old district of Transylvania, Romanian region, from which the immigrants came; organized in 1919, merged with SPERANTA-EMIGRANTUL (active) in 1955.

F-101   SIMION BARNUTIU. Chicago, Ill.

Named after Simion Barnutiu (1808-64), a Romanian leader of the 1848 Revolution in Transylvania, at that time under Austro-Hungarian rule; merged with SPERANTA, presently SPERANTA-EMIGRANTUL (active).

Indiana

F-102 MAJOR LIVIU D. TEIUSEANU (Major Liviu D. Teiuseanu). Indiana
Harbor, Ind.

Named after a Romanian hero of World War I; organized in
1919 and merged with TRANSILVANEANA (active) in 1953.

Michigan

F-103 DESTEAPTA-TE ROMANE (Awake Thee, Romanian). Detroit, Mich.

Ethnic pride name; organized in 1909; merged with HORA
UNIRII (The Unity Hora) and some other local groups, giving
birth to UNIREA ROMANILOR (active) in 1924.

F-104 FERICIREA (Happiness). Ecorse, Mich.

Self-explanatory name; organized in 1927, merged with
MARASESTI (active) in 1930.

F-105 HORA UNIRII (The Unity Hora). Highland Park, Mich.

Hora is a Romanian national dance in a circle; organized in
1913, merged with DESTEAPTA-TE ROMANE (see entry F-103)
and other local groups, bringing into existence UNIREA
ROMANILOR (active) in 1924.

F-106 INVINGEREA ROMANA (The Romanian Victory). Flint, Mich.

Organized in 1916.

F-107 PATRIOTII ROMANI AMERICANI (The Romanian American Patriots).
Highland Park, Mich.

Organized in 1952.

Minnesota

F-108 ALEXANDRU CEL BUN (Alexander the Good). South Saint Paul, Minn.

Named after a noted Romanian ruler (1400-1432) of a region
called Moldavia, in the Eastern part of Romania; organized in
1918.

F-109 ARDEALUL SI BANATUL. South Saint Paul, Minn.

Named after two Romanian regions; organized in 1929.

F-110 CAMPUL LIBERTATII (The Field of Liberty). New Duluth, Minn.

Named after a historic spot in Transylvania, where the Romanians expressed their desire for freedom during the 1848 Revolution directed against the Austro-Hungarian rulers; organized in 1916.

All three organizations from Minnesota merged and gave birth to ROMANII DIN MINNESOTA (The Romanians of Minnesota) in 1953, an organization which is still active.

Missouri

F-111 ARMONIA (Harmony). St. Louis, Mo.

Organized in 1907, sent a delegation to the inauguration of President Woodrow Wilson.

F-112 STRAINUL LIBER (The Free Alien). St. Louis, Mo.

Organized in 1913, merged with ARMONIA in 1920, under the name of ARMONIA-STRAINUL LIBER.

F-113 VASILE STROESCU. St. Louis, Mo.

Club of youth named after a Romanian leader; organized in 1911, merged with NICOLAE FILIPESCU, neighboring society honoring a prominent Romanian politician, in 1916, and then with ARMONIA in 1917.

Ohio

F-114 BIHOREANA. Lorain, Ohio.

Named after Bihor Mountains in Transylvania, Romania; organized in 1912, merged with PATRIA ROMANA (Romanian Fatherland) in 1939.

F-115 CARMEN SYLVA. Cleveland, Ohio.

Named after Queen Elizabeth of Romania (1843-1916), wife of the first Romanian monarch Carol I, whose pen name was Carmen Sylva; organized in 1904; merged with CARPATINA (active) in 1925.

F-116 CARPATI (The Carpathians). Canton, Ohio.

Named after the Carpathian Mountains of Romania; organized in 1935, merged with TRAIAN SI IULIU MANIU (active) in 1953.

F-117 CONCORDIA (Concord). Cleveland, Ohio.

Organized in 1910, merged with CARPATINA (active) in 1913.

F-118 DAIANA. Cleveland, Ohio.

Name without ethnic significance; organized in 1916, merged with DR. ANGELESCU (see entry F-119) in 1925.

F-119 DR. ANGELESCU. Cleveland, Ohio.

Named after a noted Romanian politician; organized in 1918, merged with CARPATINA (active) in 1928.

F-120 DRAPELUL ROMAN (The Romanian Flag). Struthers, Ohio.

Patriotic name; organized in 1914, merged with APOLZANA (active) in the same year.

F-121 INVIEREA (Resurrection). Martins Ferry, Ohio.

Allusion to Romanian revival on American soil; organized in 1906.

F-122 LUDOSANA. Niles, Ohio.

Named after Ludos, a locality in Transylvania, Romania, where the immigrants came from; organized in 1919, merged with IZVORUL (active) in 1925.

F-123 LUMINA ZILEI (The Light of the Day). Newark, Ohio.

Organized in 1906, merged with DACIA TRAIANA (active) in 1908.

F-124 PLUGARUL ROMAN (Romanian Ploughman). Youngstown, Ohio.

Organized in 1914; merged with UNIREA ROMANA (Romanian Unity) in 1928, giving birth to UNIREA SI PLUGARUL (active).

F-125 PRINTUL NICOLAE (Prince Nicholas). Bridgeport, Ohio.

Named after Prince Nicholas (1904-78), son of late King Ferdinand of Romania; organized in 1919, merged with IN- VIEREA in 1924.

F-126 REGELE FERDINAND I AL ROMANIEI (King Ferdinand I of Romania). Alliance, Ohio.

Named after King Ferdinand (1865-1927), the second Romanian monarch; organized in 1914, merged with UNIREA ROMANO- TRANSILVANEANA (active) in 1929.

F-127 RENASTEREA (Rebirth). Cincinnati, Ohio.

Organized in 1913, merged with DACIA in 1932, under DACIA SI RENASTEREA (active).

F-128 ROMANII DIN CLEVELAND (The Romanians of Cleveland). Cleveland, Ohio.

Organized in 1950; merged with CARPATINA (active) in 1955 after years of negotiations.

F-129 ROMANUL ARDELEAN (The Romanian of Ardeal). Cleveland, Ohio.

Ardeal has been another name for Transylvania; organized in 1917, merged with DR. ANGELESCU in 1918.

F-130 SFANTA MARIA (Saint Mary). Cleveland, Ohio.

Organized in 1908, merged with CARPATINA (active) in 1925.

F-131 SILISTRA. Girard, Ohio.

Named after a Romanian locality on the Danube; organized in 1919, merged with IZVORUL (active) in 1925.

F-132 UNIREA ROMANA ARDELEANA (The Romanian Ardelean Unity). Alliance, Ohio.

Ardeal and Transylvania are synonyms; organized in 1906, merged with UNIREA ROMANA TRANSILVANEANA (active) in 1909.

F-133 VASILE STROESCU. Cleveland, Ohio.

Named after a Romanian leader; organized in 1912, merged with CARPATINA (active) in 1925.

Pennsylvania

F-134 AURORA (Dawn). South Bethlehem, Pa.

Organized in 1918, merged with ADEVARUL in 1921, giving birth to ADEVARUL-AURORA (active).

F-135 FIII ROMANIEI (Romania's Sons). South Bethlehem, Pa.

Organized in 1921, merged with ADEVARUL -AURORA (active) in 1929.

F-136 NEGRU VODA. McKees Rocks, Pa.

Named after a locality from Dobrogea, Southern Romania; organized in 1913, merged with VULTURUL (active) in 1931.

F-137 ROMANIA MARE (Greater Romania). Universal, Pa.

> When the regions of Bessarabia, Bucovina, and Transylvania, (previously under foreign rule) were reunited with the rest of Romanian territory after World War I, Romania received the name of Greater Romania; organized in 1915, merged with VULTURUL (active) in 1931.

F-138 UNIREA ROMANA (Romanian Unity). Erie, Pa.

> Organized in 1905, merged with ULPIA TRAIANA (active) in 1910.

West Virginia

F-139 BUCURESTI (Bucharest). Whitman, W. Va.

> Named after the capital of Romania; organized in 1917, merged with MINERII ROMANI (see entry F-140) in 1922.

F-140 MINERII ROMANI (The Romanian Miners). Whitman, W. Va.

> Organized in 1922, and merged with BUCURESTI in the same year, under the name of MINERII ROMANI-BUCURESTI.

Retrospective Independent Organizations in New York City

F-141 DORUL (Yearning). New York City.

> The name implies the yearning after the land of origin; organized in 1903; functioned as a cultural, philanthropic, and social organization for several decades.

F-143 SONS OF ROMANIA. New York City..

> Organized in 1932 to maintain close ties with Romania and preserve Romanian ethnic values in America.

ROMANIAN MACEDONIAN ORGANIZATIONS

F-144 FARSAROTUL. New York City.

> Organized in 1903; had been the largest Macedo-Romanian organization in America.

F-145 MUZICHEARUL. New York City.

> Organized in 1923.

Organizations and Institutions

F-146 PERIVOLEA.   New York City.

Organized in 1909.

F-147 UNIREA.   New York City.

Organized in 1909; the name means unity.

F-148 VITOLIA.   New York City.

Organized in 1944.

NOTE: All organizations, except UNIREA, were named after native places in Macedonia (Greece and Albania) where the members came from.   They spoke a Romanian dialect called Macedo-Romanian, and had various branches in places other than New York City.   Their aim was fraternal, insurance, cultural, and charitable.

G. ROMANIAN-AMERICAN AND CANADIAN CHURCHES

This directory encompasses 105 Romanian American and Canadian churches of three denominations: Baptist, Catholic (Eastern Rite), and Orthodox.

The churches are arranged alphabetically within each denomination and locality, as well as administrative units--deaneries--whenever such were defined by the respective denominations.

For all churches, besides names and addresses, the year of establishment is mentioned whenever known. Also, in some cases, names of church designers, architects, or painters of icons are added.

Such an arrangement and annotations facilitate a better comprehension of Romanian ethnic aspects, and easier contacts between the researcher and the churches of interest.

ROMANIAN-AMERICAN BAPTIST CHURCHES

California

G-1 ROMANIAN BAPTIST CHURCH. 3759 East Fifty-seventh Street, Maywood, Los Angeles, Calif. 90058.

Illinois

G-2 LAKEVIEW BAPTIST CHURCH. 2622 North Ashland Street, Chicago, Ill. 60614.

G-3 ROMANIAN BAPTIST CHURCH. 5213 West Potomac Avenue, Chicago, Ill. 60651.

G-4 ROMANIAN PENTACOSTAL BAPTIST CHURCH. 3140 West Lawrence Avenue, Chicago, Ill. 60625.

Michigan

G-5   ROMANIAN BAPTIST CHURCH.   19447 Grandville Avenue, Detroit,
      Mich. 48219.

G-6   ROMANIAN BAPTIST CHURCH.   Oakland Boulevard, Detroit, Mich.
      48203.

G-7   ROMANIAN BAPTIST CHURCH.   17816 Woodward Avenue, Detroit,
      Mich. 48203.

New York

G-8   ROMANIAN BAPTIST CHURCH.   1915 Linden Boulevard, Ridgewood,
      N.Y. 11423.

Ohio

G-9   ROMANIAN BAPTIST CHURCH.   167 Oakland Avenue, Akron, Ohio
      44310.

G-10 ROMANIAN BAPTIST CHURCH.   1416 West Fifty-seventh Street, Cleve-
      land, Ohio 44103.

NOTE: Some churches may have changed their address. For latest changes,
one should check with the Romanian Baptist Association of the United States
and Canada (see entry F-10).

ROMANIAN CATHOLIC (EASTERN RITE) PARISHES IN AMERICA

Diocese of Cleveland

G-11 MOST HOLY TRINITY PARISH. 2650 East Ninety-third Street, Cleve-
      land, Ohio 44104. Organized December 15, 1912.

G-12 ST. BASIL'S CHURCH. Gary Avenue and East Thirty-first Street,
      Lorain, Ohio 44055. Organized June 9, 1918.

G-13 ST. HELENA'S PARISH. 1365 West Sixty-fifth Street, Cleveland, Ohio
      44102. Organized November 15, 1905; oldest Romanian Catholic parish
      in America.

Archdiocese of Detroit

G-14 ST. JOHN'S CHURCH. 20521 Woodward Avenue, Detroit, Mich. 48203. Organized August 15, 1915.

G-15 ST. MARY'S CHURCH. 801 South Military, Dearborn, Mich. 48124. Organized December 25, 1925.

Diocese of Erie

G-16 ST. GEORGE'S CHURCH. 1711 Plum Street, Erie, Pa. Organized December 16, 1917.

G-17 ST. JOHN'S CHURCH. Morefield Road, Sharon (Hickory Township), Pa. Organized May 3, 1908.

Diocese of Gary

G-18 ST. DEMETRIUS' CHURCH. 3801 Butternut Street, East Chicago, Ind. 46312. Organized September 10, 1914.

G-19 ST. NICHOLAS' CHURCH. 4301 Olcott Avenue, East Chicago, Ind. 46312. Organized February 23, 1913.

Archdiocese of Los Angeles

G-20 DESCENT OF THE HOLY SPIRIT PARISH. 2911 San Fernando Road, Los Angeles, Calif. 90065. Organized in 1976.

Diocese of Pittsburgh

G-21 ST. MARY'S CHURCH, 318 Twenty-sixty Street, McKeesport, Pa. 15132. Organized March 1918.

Diocese of Rockford

G-22 ST. GEORGE'S PARISH, 720 Rural Street, Auroa, Ill. 60505. Organized in 1955.

G-23 ST. MICHAEL'S CHURCH. 603 North Lincoln Avenue, Aurora, Ill. 60505. Organized in 1908.

Diocese of Trenton

G-24   ST. BASIL'S CHURCH.   238 Adeline Street, Trenton, N.J.   08611.
Organized in 1909.

G-25   ST. MARY'S PARISH.   180 Alden Avenue, Roebling, N.J.   08554.
Organized May 30, 1915.

Diocese of Youngstown

G-26   ST. GEORGE'S CHURCH.   1121 Forty-fourth Street, N.E., Canton,
Ohio   44714.   Organized in 1912.

G-27   ST. MARY'S CHURCH.   75 South Prospect Street, Youngstown, Ohio
44506.   Organized in 1906.

G-28   ST. THEODORE'S CHURCH.   820 South Linden Street, Alliance, Ohio
44601.   Organized August 10, 1908.

NOTE: All Romanian Catholic (Eastern Rite) parishes are served by Romanian
priests, but they fall under the jurisdiction of various local bishops, none of
whom is Romanian.   Romanian American Catholics have expressed a desire to
have their own bishop, but so far their petition has not been solved positively
by the Vatican.

ROMANIAN ORTHODOX PARISHES IN AMERICA AND CANADA

Romanian Orthodox Episcopate of America Jurisdiction

OHIO AND WESTERN PENNSYLVANIA DEANERY

G-29   THE HOLY CROSS CHURCH.   950 Maple Drive, Hermitage, Pa.   16146.
Founded September 12, 1906; architect: Arsene Rousseau, iconostasis
painted by John Terzis.

G-30   THE HOLY CROSS MISSION CHURCH.   332 Lee Avenue, Weirton,
W. Va.   26062.   No church building; affiliated with the Holy Cross
Church of Sharon, Pennsylvania.

G-31   THE HOLY RESURRECTION CHURCH.   1836 North Road, N.E., Warren,
Ohio   44483.   Founded April 15, 1917.

G-32   THE HOLY TRINITY CHURCH.   626 Wick Avenue, Youngstown, Ohio
44502.   Founded February 28, 1906; architect: Arsene Rousseau.

G-33 THE PRESENTATION OF OUR LORD CHURCH. 3365 Ridgewood Road, Akron, Ohio 44313. Founded February 15, 1914; icons painted by Ilie Hasigan.

G-34 SAINT ELIAS CHURCH. 425 Cherry Way, Ellwood City, Pa. 16117. Founded May 17, 1914; iconostasis painted by Ioan Hotia.

G-35 ST. GEORGE'S CHURCH. 144 30th Street, N.W., Canton, Ohio 44709. Founded September 29, 1912; iconostasis designed by Ovid Coatu.

G-36 ST. JOHN CHRISOSTOM CHURCH. 135 South Chestnut Street, Niles, Ohio 44460. Founded 1926.

G-37 ST. JOHN THE BAPTIST CHURCH. 1125 Pennsylvania Avenue, Erie, Pa. 16503. Founded January 10, 1909.

G-38 ST. JOHN THE EVANGELIST CHURCH. 261 South Lundy Avenue, Salem, Ohio 44460. Founded December 4, 1926.

G-39 ST. MARY'S (FALLING ASLEEP OF THE EVER VIRGIN MARY) CHURCH. 3256 Warren Road, Cleveland, Ohio 44111. Founded August 28, 1904; the oldest Romanian Orthodox Church in America; architect: Haralambie Georgescu; iconostasis designed by the architect and painted by Elie Cristo-Loveanu.

ATLANTIC SEABOARD DEANERY

G-40 THE DESCENT OF THE HOLY GHOST CHURCH. 323 Ashbourne Road, Elkins Park, Pa. 19117. Founded in 1911; iconostasis designed by George Ciukurescu, icons painted by John Bogdan.

G-41 THE HOLY CROSS CHURCH. 5150 Leesburg Pike, Alexandria, Va. 22303. Founded 1913.

G-42 THE HOLY TRINITY CHURCH. 10300 Northwest Thirty-sixth Place, Miami, Fla. 33147. Founded November 20, 1956.

G-43 ST. DIMITRIE CHURCH. 579 Clinton Avenue, Bridgeport, Conn. 06605. Founded in 1927; iconostasis painted by Alexandru Seceni.

G-44 ST. DUMITRU CHURCH. 50 West Eighty-ninth Street, New York, N.Y. 10024. Interior chapel built in 1939; iconostasis, furniture, and painting by Vasile Irimie, Alexandru Seceni, and Elie Cristo-Loveanu.

Churches

G-45 ST. JOHN THE BAPTIST CHURCH. 501 East School Street, Woonsocket, R.I. 02895. Founded December 1, 1912.

G-46 THREE HIERARCHS CHURCH. 68-59 Sixtieth Lane and Catalpa Avenue, Ridgewood, N.Y. 11227. Founded August 30, 1969.

G-47 THE DESCENT OF THE HOLY GHOST. 750 West Sixty-first Avenue, Merrillville, Ind. 46410. Founded October 11, 1908; iconostasis painted by Fr. Nathaniel Popp and Fr. Mark Forsberg.

G-48 THE HOLY NATIVITY CHURCH. 6352 North Paulina Street, Chicago, Ill. 60660. Founded May 21, 1939.

G-49 THE HOLY RESURRECTION CHURCH. San Francisco, Calif. Mission Church; no church building. Founded December 10, 1964.

G-50 THE HOLY TRINITY CHURCH. 3315 Verdugo Road. Los Angeles, Calif. 90065. Founded June 25, 1939; icons painted by Mrs. George Sabau.

G-51 ST. ANDREW'S CHURCH. 1311 North Twenty-fifth Street, Terre Haute, Ind. 47803. Founded April 21, 1918.

MIDWEST AND WESTERN DEANERY

G-52 ST. MARY (FALLING ASLEEP OF THE EVER VIRGIN MARY) CHURCH. 4225 North Central Avenue, Chicago, Ill. 60634. Founded December 19, 1911; iconostasis by John Terzis.

G-53 ST. MARY (THE FALLING ASLEEP OF THE EVER VIRGIN MARY) CHURCH. Atwater and Woodridge Street, St. Paul, Minn. 55117. Founded May 18, 1913.

G-54 SS. ARCHANGELS MICHAEL AND GABRIEL CHURCH. 2902 Evans Street, Fort Wayne, Ind. 46805. Founded 1912; uses the building of the Ukrainian Orthodox Church.

G-55 SS. CONSTANTIN AND HELENA CHURCH. 3237 West Sixteenth Street, Indianapolis, Ind. 46222. Founded June 12, 1910.

G-56 ST. THOMAS THE APOSTLE CHURCH. 6501 Nottingham Avenue, St. Louis, MO. 63109. Founded May 5, 1935.

MICHIGAN AND EASTERN CANADA DEANERY

G-57 THE DESCENT OF THE HOLY GHOST CHURCH. 7835 East Lafayette

Street, Detroit, Mich. 48214. Founded September 10, 1917; iconostasis painted by C. Trandaphillou.

G-58 ST. GEORGE'S CATHEDRAL. 18405 West Nine Mile Road, Southfield, Mich. 48075. Founded March 1912; architect: Georgescu-Pirchser; iconostasis built and painted by Alexandru Seceni.

G-59 ST. NICHOLAS CHURCH. 20480 John R, Detroit, Mich. 48203. Founded November 15, 1955.

G-60 ST. MARY (THE NATIVITY OF THE EVER VIRGIN MARY) CHURCH. 2522 Grey Tower Road, Jackson, Mich. 49201. Founded in 1956; iconostasis designed and built by Constantin Antonovici; icons painted by Elie Cristo-Loveanu.

G-61 ST. SIMEON'S CHURCH. 920 West Seven Mile Road, Detroit, Mich. 48203. Founded October 18, 1941.

G-62 SS. PETER AND PAUL CHURCH. 750 North Beech Daly, Dearborn Heights, Mich. 48127. Founded June 15, 1929; iconostasis designed and painted by Alexandru Seceni.

ONTARIO-CANADA DEANERY

G-63 ST. GEORGE CHURCH. 247 Rosethorn Avenue, Toronto, Ontario. Founded May 16, 1954; architect: Constantin Marutescu; iconostasis designed by the same.

G-64 ST. JOHN THE BAPTIST CHURCH. 335 Lancaster Street, Kitchener, Ontario. Founded July 30, 1967; iconostasis designed by Andrei Carnician.

WESTERN CANADA DEANERY

G-65 THE DESCENT OF THE HOLY GHOST CHURCH. 504 Sixth Avenue, East, Assiniboia, Saskatchewan. Founded in 1957; iconostasis painted by Mrs. George Sabau.

G-66 THE HOLY TRINITY CHURCH. Mac Nutt, Saskatchewan. Founded in 1903.

G-67 ST. ELIAS, THE PROPHET CHURCH. Lennard, Manitoba. Founded in 1902.

G-68 ST. GEORGE CHURCH. Dysart, Saskatchewan. Founded in 1905; architect: Lockie Jonescu.

G-69 ST. GEORGE CHURCH. 2005 Edgar Street, Regina, Saskatchewan. Founded in 1914.

G-70 ST. GEORGE CHURCH. 123 Harvard Avenue. Winnipeg, Manitoba. Founded November 22, 1961.

G-71 ST. JOHN THE BAPTIST CHURCH. Shell Valley, Manitoba. Founded in 1919.

G-72 ST. MARY (THE NATIVITY OF THE EVER VIRGIN MARY) CHURCH. First Street and Seventh Avenue, S.E., Calgary, Alberta. Founded November 26, 1969; no church building, uses "Paget Hall" space.

G-73 ST. NICHOLAS CHURCH. 1756 St. John Street, Regina, Saskatchewan. Founded 1902; the oldest Romanian Orthodox Church on the North American continent.

G-74 SS. PETER AND PAUL CHURCH. Canora, Saskatchewan. Founded in 1903; together with Ukrainians of Eastern Orthodox faith.

G-75 SS. PETER AND PAUL CHURCH. Flintoft, Saskatchewan. Founded in 1911.

Romanian Orthodox Missionary Archdiocese Jurisdiction

MIDDLE WEST AND WESTERN U.S.A. DEANERY

G-76 HOLY CROSS ROMANIAN ORTHODOX CHURCH. 3221 R Street, Omaha, Neb. 68107.

G-77 ROMANIAN ORTHODOX MISSION. 6904 Orchard Avenue, Bell, Calif. 90201. No church building.

MICHIGAN AND CENTRAL U.S.A. DEANERY

G-78 ANNUNCIATION ROMANIAN ORTHODOX CATHEDRAL. 4074 West 204th Street, Fairview Park, Ohio 44126.

G-79 HOLY TRINITY ROMANIAN ORTHODOX CHURCH. 1771 East State Fair, Detroit, Mich. 48203.

G-80 ST. ANDREW ROMANIAN ORTHODOX CHURCH. Cincinnati, Ohio. Affiliated; served by a priest from a neighboring parish.

G-81 ST. GEORGE'S ROMANIAN CHURCH. 19959 Riopelle, Detroit, Mich. 48203. Affiliated.

G-82 ST. GEORGE THE NEW ROMANIAN ORTHODOX CHURCH. 17601 Wentworth Avenue, Lansing, Ill. 60438. Founded in 1906.

G-83 ST. MARY'S ROMANIAN ORTHODOX PARISH. Fort Wayne, Ind. Served by a priest from Lansing, Illinois.

NEW YORK AND EASTERN U.S.A. DEANERY

G-84 HOLY TRINITY ROMANIAN ORTHODOX CHURCH. 723 North Bodine Street, Philadelphia, Pa. 19123.

G-85 ST. MICHAEL ROMANIAN ORTHODOX CHURCH. 16 Romanian Avenue, Southbridge, Mass. 01550. Founded in 1924.

G-86 ST. NICHOLAS ROMANIAN ORTHODOX CHURCH. 76-09 Thirty-fourth Avenue, Jackson Heights, N.Y. 11372.

ONTARIO AND EASTERN CANADA DEANERY

G-87 DESCENT OF THE HOLY GHOST ROMANIAN ORTHODOX CHURCH. 1480 Cadillac Street, Windsor, Ontario.

G-88 HOLY RESURRECTION ROMANIAN ORTHODOX CHURCH. 19 Murray Street, West., Hamilton, Ontario. Founded in 1916.

G-89 ST. GEORGE ROMANIAN ORTHODOX CATHEDRAL. 1960 Tecumseh Road, East, Windsor, Ontario. Founded in 1918.

G-90 ST. JOHN THE BAPTIST ROMANIAN ORTHODOX CHURCH. 1841 Masson Street, Montreal, Quebec. Founded in 1918.

G-91 ST. MARY ROMANIAN ORTHODOX CHURCH. 98 Eighth Street, Timmins, Ontario. Founded in 1933.

G-92 SS. PETER AND PAUL ROMANIAN ORTHODOX PARISH. 32 Joseph Street, Kitchener, Ontario.

SASKATCHEWAN AND WESTERN CANADA DEANERY

All churches of Saskatchewan are served by the same priest; all churches of Alberta are served by the same priest.

G-93 ASCENSION OF OUR LORD ROMANIAN ORTHODOX CHURCH. Elm Spring, Saskatchewan.

G-94 DESCENT OF THE HOLY GHOST CHURCH. Manning-Peace River, Alberta.

G-95 DESCENT OF THE HOLY GHOST ROMANIAN ORTHODOX CHURCH. Pierceland, Saskatchewan. Founded in 1934.

G-96 DESCENT OF THE HOLY GHOST ROMANIAN ORTHODOX CHURCH. Hamlin, Alberta. Founded in 1915.

G-97 HOLY CROSS ROMANIAN ORTHODOX CHURCH. Malin, Alberta.

G-98 HOLY TRANSFIGURATION ROMANIAN ORTHODOX CHURCH. Wood Mountain, Saskatchewan.

G-100 ST. JOHN THE BAPTIST ROMANIAN ORTHODOX CHURCH. Marcelin, Saskatchewan.

G-101 ST. MARY ROMANIAN ORTHODOX CHURCH. Boian (Willingdon), Alberta. Founded in 1905.

G-102 ST. MARY ROMANIAN ORTHODOX CHURCH. Hairy Hill, Alberta. Founded in 1911.

G-103 ST. MARY ROMANIAN ORTHODOX CHURCH. Kayville, Saskatchewan.

G-104 SS. CONSTANTINE AND HELEN ROMANIAN ORTHODOX PARISH. Edmonton, Alberta.

G-105 SS. PETER AND PAUL ROMANIAN ORTHODOX CHURCH. Kayville, Saskatchewan.

NOTE: Although the Romanian Orthodox Episcopate of America and the Romanian Orthodox Missionary Diocese are independent church bodies, their dogma and liturgy are the same.

H. ROMANIAN-AMERICAN AND ROMANIAN-CANADIAN ACTIVE AND RETROSPECTIVE PERIODICALS

This directory lists twenty-seven active and ninety-five retrospective newspaper and periodical publications in the United States and Canada. They are arranged by country in alphabetical order, and for each item the following information is provided:

> title (with translation in English when needed)
> name of publisher or editor
> place of publication
> date of publication (year or years)
> frequency
> nature of publication, orientation
> miscellaneous data (if needed)

ACTIVE ROMANIAN-AMERICAN PERIODICALS

H-1   ACTIUNEA ROMANEASCA (The Romanian Action). The Romanian National Committee. P.O. Box A-111, Radio City Station, New York, N.Y. 10019. 1970-- . Quarterly. In Romanian.

> Anti-communist; preservation of Romanian heritage and coverage of contributions made to Western civilization by Romanians, in the fields of science, culture, art, and so forth.

H-2   AMERICA: ROMANIAN NEWS. Union and League of Romanian Societies of America. 2121 West 117th Street, Cleveland, Ohio 44111. 1906-- . Monthly. In English and Romanian.

> U.L.R.S.A. interests; preservation of Romanian national consciousness in American in Canada. Oldest and most widely circulated newspaper in America and Canada.

H-3   AMERICAN ROMANIAN REVIEW. American Romanian Heritage Foundation, Inc. 17313 Puritas Avenue, Cleveland, Ohio 44135. 1977-- . Bimonthly. In English, with some materials in Romanian.

> Continues the tradition of the NEW PIONEER (retrospective), having the same editor, Theodore Andrica.

Active and Retrospective Periodicals

H-4   CALENDARUL CREDINTA (Credinta Almanac). Romanian Orthodox Missionary Archdiocese in America. 19965 Riopelle, Detroit, Mich. 48203. 1961-- . Annual. In Romanian and English.

An almanac, supplement to the newspaper CREDINTA (active). Religious calendar, main events in parishes, ties with Romania. Profusely illustrated.

H-5   CALENDARUL SOLIA (Solia Almanac). 11341 Woodward Avenue, Detroit, Mich. 48202. Romanian Orthodox Episcopate of America. 1935-- . Annual. In Romanian and English.

An almanac, supplement to the newspaper SOLIA (active). Religious calendar, main events in parishes, directory of parishes and serving priests, contributions to America. Profusely illustrated.

H-6   CALENDARUL ZIARULUI AMERICA (Almanac of America Newspaper). Union and League of Romanian Societies of America. 2121 West 117th Street, Cleveland, Ohio 44111. 1906-- . Annual. In Romanian and English.

An almanac, supplement to the newspaper AMERICA (active). Main events in the life of U.L.R.S.A., historical articles, contributions made by Romanians in America and Canada, directory of affiliated organizations, Romanian heritage. Profusely illustrated.

H-7   COMUNIUNEA ROMANEASCA (The Romanian Communion). Gheorghe Alexe, business manager of CREDINTA (active). 19965 Riopelle, Detroit, Mich. 48203. 1973-- . Monthly. In Romanian and English.

Culture and art, closer ties with Romania, news from this country.

H-8   CREDINTA (The Belief). Romanian Orthodox Missionary Archdiocese in America. 19965 Riopelle, Detroit, Mich. 48203. 1952-- . In Romanian.

Religious and parish news, general information and comments.

H-9   DREPTATEA (Justice). Romanian private group claiming to be independent. P.O. Box 54, Time Square Station, New York, N.Y. 10036. 1973-- . Monthly. In Romanian.

News from Romanian American and Canadian communities, literary contributions, commentaries.

H-10 DRUM (Path). John Halmaghi, private publisher. 215 Valley Drive, Pittsburgh, Pa. 15215. 1964-- . Quarterly. In Romanian.

Historical, literary, political news regarding Romanians from all over the world.

H-11 EXILUL SOLIDAR (The Solidary Exile). Petre Mihail, private publisher. 1651 Second Avenue, Box 65, New York, N.Y. 10028. 1972-- . Irregular. In Romanian.

Anti-Communist; feelings expressed by a group of Romanian refugees and exiles from various countries.

H-12 FARUL MANTUIRII (The Lighthouse of Redemption). Romanian Baptist Church. 167 Oakdale Avenue, Akron, Ohio 44302. 1973-- . Quarterly. In Romanian. Mimeographed.

Religious news.

H-13 LUMINATORUL (The Illuminator). Romanian Baptist Association of America. c/o Rev. Danila Pascu, 9410 Clifton Boulevard, Cleveland, Ohio 44102. 1926-- . Monthly. In Romanian.

Religious education and news from churches; literary materials, youth achievements.

H-14 MICROMAGAZINE. Marius Luigi, private publisher. 18-47 Twenty-sixth Road, Astoria, N.Y. 11102. 1972-- . Monthly. In Romanian.

General information, political commentaries, health, sport, humor, and other columns. Extensive publication, illustrated.

H-15 PORUNCA VREMII (The Command of Time). George F.A. Boian, private publisher. 300 East Ninety-first Street, New York, N.Y. 10028. 1968-- . Monthly. In Romanian. Mimeographed.

Anti-Communist; short articles and comments destined for Romanian refugees and exiles from American, Canada, and other countries.

H-16 ROMANIA DEMOCRATA (Democratic Romania). J.T. Faget, private publisher. 47-43 Forty-third Street, Woodside, N.Y. 11377. 1945-- . Irregular. In Romanian. Mimeographed.

Anti-Communist; short articles political and literary.

H-17 ROMANIAN PHILATELIC STUDIES. Miron Abramovici, private publisher. 209 Bergen Street, Somerset, N.J. 08873. 1977-- . Quarterly. In English.

Short studies and news regarding Romanian stamps; of interest to stamp collectors.

H-18 ROMANIAN SOURCES. University of Pittsburgh Libraries and American Romanian Institute for Research, Inc. 261 Hillman Library, University of Pittsburgh, Pa. 15260. 1975-- . Semiannual. In English.

Romanian culture and civilization; Romanian heritage in America; studies, book reviews, comments; scholarly. Indexed in HISTO-RICAL ABSTRACTS.

H-19 SEMANATORUL (The Sower). Romanian American Baptist Group. 5213 Potomac Avenue, Chicago, Ill. 60651. 1970-- . Bimonthly. In Romanian.

Religious education, comments, poetry, youth activities.

H-20 SOLIA (The Herald). The Romanian Orthodox Episcopate of America. 11341 Woodward Avenue, Detroit, Mich. 48302. 1935-- . Monthly. In Romanian and English.

Religious and parish life news, ladies auxiliaries and youth activities; Romanian heritage and culture in America and and Canada. Circulates both in America and Canada.

H-21 UNIREA (Unity). Association of Romanian Catholics of America. 4309 Olcott Avenue, East Chicago, Indiana 46312. 1950-- . Monthly. In Romanian and English.

Religious and general news; parish activities, youth life and accomplishments, book reviews, comments. Indexed in INDEX TO CATHOLIC LITERATURE.

H-22 UNIREA ALMANAC. Association of Romanian Catholics of America. 4309 Olcott Avenue, East Chicago, Ind. 46312. 1950-- . Annual. In Romanian and English.

An almanac, supplement to the newspaper UNIREA (active). Religious calendar, main events, historical, political and cultural articles; preservation of Romanian Catholic heritage. Profusely illustrated; directory of parishes and priests.

H-23 VIATA IN CHRISTOS (Life in Christ). Romanian Christian Baptist Institute. 348 Cole Avenue and Sherman Street, Akron, Ohio 44301. 1975. Quarterly. In Romanian. Mimeographed.

Religious newsletter.

ACTIVE ROMANIAN-CANADIAN PERIODICALS

H-24 CUVANTUL ROMANESC (The Romanian Word). George Balasu, private publisher. P.O. Box 4217 Station D, Hamilton, Ontario. 1976-- . Monthly. In Romanian.

General news, cultural, religious, political articles of various orientations; sport, health, humor, and other columns geared to a wide range of readers. Claims to be the largest Romanian newspaper in the Western world.

H-25 ECOURI ROMANESTI (Romanian Echoes). Romanian Canadian Association of Ontario. 1862 Eglinton Avenue West, Toronto, M6E 234. 1973. Monthly. In Romanian.

General information, Romanian Canadian life; close ties with Romania.

H-26 VESTITORUL ROMAN CANADIAN (The Romanian Canadian Messenger). Rev. Fr. Dumitru D. Ichim, Sts. Peter and Paul Romanian Orthodox Parish. 71 Vanier Drive, Apt. 201, Kitchener, Ontario. 1973-- . Quarterly. In Romanian.

Religious and parish news, close ties with Romania. Falls under the jurisdiction of the Romanian Orthodox Missionary Archdiocese of America.

ROMANIAN GOVERNMENT PUBLICATION IN AMERICA AND CANADA

H-27 ROMANIAN BULLETIN. Romanian Library. 200 East Thirty-eighth Street, New York, N.Y. 10016. 1968-- . Monthly. In English.

General news on Romania and its achievements; some materials are on Romanian Americans or Canadians.

RETROSPECTIVE ROMANIAN-AMERICAN PERIODICALS

H-28 ADEVARUL (The Truth). Union of the Romanian Greek-Catholic Societies of America. Cleveland, Ohio. 1924. Monthly. In Romanian.

Religious news.

H-29 ADEVARUL (The Truth). Olimpiu Cloanta, private publisher. Gary, Ind. 1944-45. Irregular. In Romanian.

Opposed to the U.L.R.S.A.

H-30 ALLRIGHT. Nicolae Zamfirescu and M. Lazin, private publishers. Cleveland, Ohio. 1908-9. Monthly. Later bimonthly. In Romanian (despite its title).

Literary and humorous.

H-31   AMERICA LITERARA (Literary America). Union and League of Romanian
Societies of America. Cleveland, Ohio. 1917-18. Monthly. In
Romanian.

> General and cultural information. Appeared as a supplement
> to America.

H-32   AMERICA NOASTRA (Our America). Union and League of Romanian
Societies of America. Cleveland, Ohio. 1933. Irregular. In Romanian.

> U.L.R.S.A. internecine fights. Had only a short existence.

H-33   BIBLIOTECA ANDREI SAGUNA (The Andrei Saguna Library). Vasile
Musi, private publisher. Cleveland, Ohio. 1950. Irregular. In
Romanian.

> Cultural news. Andrei Saguna was a prominent Romanian
> bishop and cultural activist in Transylvania during the nine-
> teenth century. The publication had only a brief existence.

H-34   BISERICA (The Church). Fr. Alexandru Bocioaga, private publisher.
Indianapolis, Ind. 1936. Irregular. In Romanian.

> Religious news.

H-35   BRAZDA STRABUNA (Ancient Land). Vasile Basarab, private publisher.
Shapsville, Pa. 1960-- ? Bimonthly. In Romanian.

> Anti-Communist.

H-36   BULETINUL MILITAR (Military Bulletin). Col. Dan Ivanovici, private
publisher. 1952-62. Monthly. In Romanian.

> Military events from Romania and Eastern Europe.

H-37   BULETINUL OFICIAL (The Official Bulletin). Union of the Romanian
Greek-Catholic Societies of America. Cleveland, Ohio. 1924.
Quarterly. In Romanian.

> Religious news.

H-38   CALENDARUL INSTRAINATULUI (The Alien's Calendar). Iancu Roman,
private publisher. New York City. 1914. Irregular. In Romanian.

> Assorted news. Had only a brief existence.

H-39   CALICUL (The Pauper). Anonymous private publisher. Ecorse, Mich.
1934. Irregular. In Romanian.

> Humorous and pornographic. Had only a brief existence.

H-40 CALICUL (The Pauper). Anonymous private publisher. Detroit, Mich. 1936. Irregular. In Romanian.

Humorous and pornographic. Probably issued by the same publisher as entry H-39.

H-41 CALICUL AMERICAN (The American Pauper). Ioan Sufana, private publisher. Indiana Harbor, Mich. 1909-16. Irregular. In Romanian.

Defended the interests of the U.L.R.S.A. against its opponents.

H-42 CRESTINUL (The Christian). Romanian American Baptist Group. Detroit, Mich. 1917-25. Monthly. In Romanian.

Religious news and propaganda.

H-43 CROCODILUL ROMAN (The Romanian Crocodile). Teodor Andrica and Jeican, private publishers. Cleveland, Ohio. 1928. Irregular. In Romanian.

Humorous. Had only a brief existence.

H-44 CRONICA ROMANEASCA (The Romanian Chronicle). Free Europe Organization Group. Washington, D.C. 1950-57. Monthly. In Romanian.

Anti-Communist; news from Romania and Romanian refugees to the West.

H-45 CURIERUL AMERICAN (The Romanian Courier). Farsarotul and Muzicherul, Romanian Macedonian societies. New York City. 1923-24. Weekly. In Romanian and Romanian Macedonian dialect.

News regarding the Romanian Macedonian community.

H-46 CUVANTUL PACII (The Word of Peace). The Descent of the Holy Ghost Romanian Orthodox Parish. Detroit, Mich. 1937-39. Monthly. In Romanian.

Parish news.

H-47 DESTEAPTA-TE ROMANE (Awake Thee, Romanian). Iancu Roman, private publisher. New York City. 1911-16. Weekly. In Romanian.

Pro-Astro-Hungarian after the outbreak of World War I. The majority of Romanian Americans were against the Austo-Hungarian Empire, and fought for the reunification of Transylvania with Romania.

H-48 DESTEPTAREA (The Awakening). Federation of Romanian Socialists in America. Chicago, Ill.; Cleveland, Ohio; later Detroit, Mich. 1914-

38. Weekly; later bimonthly. In Romanian.

Pro-Communist. Replaced by ROMANUL AMERICAN (retro-spective).

H-49 DETROITUL (Detroit). I. Gradulescu, private publisher. Detroit, Mich. 1924. Weekly. In Romanian.

General and cultural news.

H-50 DREPTATEA (Justice). Alexandru Vernescu, private publisher. Detroit, Mich. 1922. Irregular. In Romanian.

Voice of an opposition group within U.L.R.S.A. Had only a brief existence.

H-51 DREPTATEA (Justice). Detroit, Mich. 1948. Irregular. In Romanian.

Local polemics. Had only a brief existence.

H-52 DREPTATEA (Justice). Ion Drugociu, private publisher. Detroit, Mich. 1952. Irregular. In Romanian.

Anti-Communist.

H-53 DRUM DREPT (The Right Path). Nicolae Vamasescu, private publisher. Detroit, Mich. 1943-44. Irregular. In Romanian.

General news. Had only a brief existence.

H-54 DUNAREANA (The Danubian). Dunarea Society. Detroit, Mich. 1940. Irregular. In Romanian.

Local news. The Danube crosses the Southern part of Romania. The publication had only a brief existence.

H-55 ECOUL AMERICAN (The American Echo). Lucian Marcu, private publisher. New York City. 1924. Weekly; later bimonthly. In Romanian.

General news.

H-56 ECOUL AMERICEI (America's Echo). New York City. 1904. Irregular. In Romanian.

Assorted cultural and political news. The publication had only a brief existence.

H-57 ECOUL AMERICEI (America's Echo). Nicolae Zamfirescu, private publisher. Cleveland, Ohio. 1910. Irregular. In Romanian.

Humorous.

H-58 EPISCOPIA (The Episcopate). Bishop Andrei Moldovan, private publisher. Detroit, Mich. 1951. Irregular. In Romanian.

Opposed to the Romanian Episcopate of America. Was banned by court order after only a brief existence.

H-59 ERA NOUA (New Era). Romanian Democratic Club. Youngstown, Ohio. 1935-37. Weekly. In Romanian.

Defended the interests of the U.L.R.S.A.

H-60 FAMILIA (The Family). M. Lazin, private publisher. Detroit, Mich. 1917. Monthly. In Romanian.

Family life aspects. The publication had only a brief existence.

H-61 FIII DACIEI (The Sons of Dacia). F.A. Boian, private publisher. New York City. 1937. Irregular. In Romanian.

Nationalistic and general news. Dacia was Romania's ancient name before it had been conquered by Roman Emperor Trajan in the second century A.D. The publication had only a brief existence.

H-62 FOAIA POPORULUI (The People's Paper). Gheorghe Ungureanu; later Gheorghe Stanculescu, private publishers. Cleveland, Ohio, later Detroit, Mich. 1913-57. Weekly. In Romanian.

General news; first sponsoring Romanian Catholic views, later favoring Bishop Teofil Ionescu.

H-63 GLASUL POPORULUI (The People's Voice). Gheorghe Stanculescu, private publisher. Detroit, Mich. 1956. Irregular. In Romanian.

Favored a religious group led by Bishop Teofil Ionescu. The publication had only a brief existence.

H-64 GLASUL ROMANESC (The Romanian Voice). Romania Libera Movement. Detroit, Mich. 1942-44. Weekly. In Romanian.

Promonarchist, favoring King Carol II of Romania who abdicated in 1940.

H-65 GLASUL TINERETULUI (The Voice of the Youth). Central Organization of the Romanian American Youth. Detroit, Mich. 1936-41. Monthly; later irregular. In Romanian.

News covering the interests of the younger generation of Romanian Americans. Ceased publication due to financial difficulties.

H-66   GLASUL VREMII (The Voice of the Time). Iosif Schiopul; later Fr.
Ion Podea, private publishers. Youngstown, Ohio. 1912–16. Weekly;
later irregular. In Romanian.

Opposed the U.L.R.S.A.; expressed the views of a group of
priests.

H-67   GLASUL VREMII (The Voice of the Time). The Romanian Orthodox
Church of America. Cleveland, Ohio. 1932–33. Irregular. In Romanian.

General news of interest to parishioners. The publication had
only a brief existence.

H-68   LEGEA STRAMOSEASCA (The Forefathers Law). Rev. Ioan Popovici.
Erie, Pa. 1924–36. Monthly. In Romanian.

Religious education.

H-69   LIBERTATEA (Freedom). I.N. Barbu and N. Dragos, private publishers.
Detroit, Mich. 1930. Weekly. In Romanian.

General and local news.

H-70   LIBERTATEA (Freedom). George Petrino, private publisher. Chicago,
Ill. 1952–53. Weekly; later irregular. In Romanian.

General news.

H-71   LUMEA NOUA (New World). John J. Banateanu and Gheorghe
Stanculescu, private publishers. Indianapolis, Ind. 1927. Irregular.
In Romanian.

Internecine fights within U.L.R.S.A., supporting an opposition
group. The publication had only a brief existence.

H-72   LUMINA (The Light). Association of the Romanian American Orthodox
Priests. Erie, Pa.; later Chicago, Ill. 1922–24; 1934. Irregular.
In Romanian.

Defended the rights of the Romanian Orthodox priests ordained
in America.

H-73   LUMINA (The Light). Romanian American National Committee. Cleveland, Ohio. 1945–48. Irregular. In Romanian.

Anti-Communist, fought against Communist infiltration in Romanian American organizations.

H-74   MONITORUL (The Monitor). The Romanian National Committee.
Washington, D.C. 1950–55. Bimonthly. In Romanian.

Anti-Communist and news from Romania. Replaced by
ROMANIA (retrospective).

H-75 THE NEW PIONEER. Cultural Association of Americans of Romanian
Descent. Cleveland, Ohio. 1942-48. Bimonthly; later irregular. In
English.

Romanian heritage and contributions in America. Edited by
Theodore Andrica who presently publishes AMERICAN ROMA-
NIAN REVIEW (active).

H-76 ORIZONTUL (The Horizon). John Lepa and J.W. Jones, private
publishers. Detroit, Mich. 1926. Irregular. In Romanian.

Cultural news. The publication had only a brief existence.

H-77 ORIZONTUL (The Horizon). Anonymous. Cleveland, Ohio. 1930.
Irregular. In Romanian.

Internecine fights within the U.L.R.S.A. The publication had
only a brief existence.

H-78 ORTODOXUL ROMAN (The Romanian Orthodox). Rev. Solomon Duma.
Canton, Ohio. 1918. Irregular. In Romanian.

Romanian Orthodox education. The publication had only a
brief existence.

H-79 PAMANTUL (The Land). Teodor Sitea, private publisher. East Chicago,
Ind. 1930. Irregular. In Romanian and English.

Leftist orientation. The publication had only a brief existence.

H-80 POSTA (The Mail). Hary Reich, Publisher. Cleveland, Ohio. 1924.
Irregular. In Romanian.

Advertising. The publication had only a brief existence.

H-81 POSTA ROMANA (The Romanian Mail). D. Disescu, private publisher.
Pittsburgh, Pa. 1909-10. Irregular. In Romanian.

General news.

H-82 PROGRESUL (The Progress). Constantin Harjeu, private publisher.
Detroit, Mich. 1916-17. Weekly. In Romanian.

Polemics, against the newspaper AMERICA (active).

H-83 PROGRESUL ROMAN (The Romanian Progress). Dr. Iuliu Maniu Society.
Canton, Ohio. 1924. Irregular. In Romanian.

General and cultural news.

H-84 RASUNETUL (The Echo). Christopher Gotiu, private publisher. Detroit, Mich. 1925-28. Weekly. In Romanian.

Economic problems.

H-85 RENASTEREA ROMANA (The Romanian Revival). Alexandru Landescu, private publisher. Cincinnati, Ohio. 1913. Irregular. In Romanian.

Assorted cultural and political news. The publication had only a brief existence.

H-86 ROMANIA. The Romanian National Committee. New York City. 1955-74. Monthly. In Romanian.

Anti-Communist; political and cultural news.

H-87 THE ROMANIAN BULLETIN. Sons of Romania Club. New York City. 1932-34. Irregular. In English.

Romanian American life and news from Romania.

H-88 ROMANUL (The Romanian). Rev. Fr. Epaminonda Lucaciu; later U.L.R.S.A. Cleveland, Ohio. 1905-28. Daily; later weekly. In Romanian.

Religious--Romanian Catholic; later political polemics. Also known as: LUMEA NOUA, FLAMURA, TULNICUL, and DREPTATEA in various American cities between 1910 and 1912.

H-89 ROMANUL (The Romanian). League of Free Romanians. New York City. 1951-67. Quarterly. In Romanian.

Political--anti-Communist.

H-90 ROMANUL AMERICAN (The Romanian American). Rev. Fr. Epaminonda Lucaciu, private publisher. New York City. 1910-12. Weekly. In Romanian.

Religious--Romanian Catholic.

H-91 ROMANUL AMERICAN (The Romanian American). Romanian American Movement. Detroit, Mich. 1938-67. Weekly; later monthly. In Romanian.

Pro-Communist. Replaced DESTEPTAREA (retrospective).

H-92 ROMANUL LIBER (The Free Romanian). Ioan Budai and George Pintea, private publishers. Youngstown, Ohio; later Sharon, Pa. 1936. Irregular.

General news. The publication had a brief existence.

H-93 ROMANUL LIBER (The Free Romanian). Rev. Fr. Stefan Opreanu, private publisher. Detroit, Mich. 1941-42. Monthly. In English (despite its title).

General news.

H-94 ROUMANIA. Paul Negulescu, private publisher. Chicago, Ill. 1917-18. Monthly. In English and Romanian.

Popularization of Romania and its cause during World War I.

H-95 ROUMANIA. Society of Friends of Roumania. New York City. 1928-32. Quarterly. In English.

Popularization of Romania in the United States.

H-96 SAGEATA (The Arrow). Alexandru Vernescu, private publisher. Cleveland, Ohio; later Detroit, Mich. 1922. Monthly; later irregular. In Romanian.

Political polemics. The publication had only a brief existence.

H-97 SAMANOTORUL (The Sower). Rev. Fr. Ion Podea, private publisher. Youngstown, Ohio. 1915-19. Monthly. In Romanian.

Religious-Romanian Orthodox; later leftist and anticlerical.

H-98 SEMNELE TIMPULUI (The Signs of the Time). Romanian Pentacostal Group. Dearborn, Mich. 1946-51. Monthly. In Romanian.

Religious--advocating Pentecostal belief.

H-99 SENTINELA (The Sentry). A. Lupea and Gh. Stanculescu, private publishers. Indianapolis, Ind. 1916-17. Monthly. In Romanian.

Political--pro-U.L.R.S.A.

H-100 SENTINELA (The Sentry). Granicerul Society. Detroit, Mich. 1941. Irregular. In Romanian.

Local news. The publication had only a brief existence.

H-101 SOLIA (The Herald). Neamtu-Martin and Clicherie Moraru, private publishers. Cleveland, Ohio. 1951. Irregular. In Romanian.

Religious disputes--supporting Bishop Andrei Moldovan against the leadership of the Romanian Orthodox Episcopate of America. The publication had only a brief existence before it was banned by the federal court of Cleveland.

H-102 STEAUA NOASTRA (Our Star). P. Axelrad, private publisher. New

York City. 1911-24. Weekly. In Romanian.

Publicizing owner's book store of Romanian books; some literary materials and book reviews.

H-103 TESALA (The Curry). Anonymous. Struthers, Ohio. 1929. Irregular. In Romanian.

Humorous. The publication had only a brief existence.

H-104 TRANSILVANIA (Transylvania). Romanian Orthodox National Committee. Youngstown, Ohio. 1917-18. Weekly. In Romanian.

Political--concerning U.L.R.S.A. internecine fights.

H-105 TRAZNETUL (The Thunderbolt). Vasile Basarab, private publisher. Shapsville, Pa. 1959-60. Bimonthly. In Romanian.

Anti-Communist. Changed name to BRAZDA STRABUNA (retrospective).

H-106 TRIBUNA (The Tribune). Liviu Pascu, private publisher. Cleveland, Ohio. 1903. In Romanian. Irregular.

General news. The first Romanian newspaper in America, it had only a brief existence.

H-107 TRIBUNA (The Tribune). Rev. Fr. Octavian Muresan, private publisher. Chicago, Ill. 1915-18. Weekly. In Romanian.

Religious--Romanian Orthodox.

H-108 TRIBUNA (The Tribune). Detroit, Mich. 1923-24. Daily; weekly. In Romanian.

General and local news.

H-109 TRIBUNA (The Tribune). Neamtu-Martin and Glicherie Moraru, private publishers. Detroit, Mich. 1951-52. Monthly. In Romanian.

Religious, opposing the Romanian Orthodox Episcopate of America. Replaced SOLIA and EPISCOPIA, (both retrospective).

H-110 TRIBUNA ROMANA (The Romanian Tribune). Nicolae Drugociu, private publisher. Detroit, Mich. 1924-33. Monthly. In Romanian.

Anti-Communist and religious education.

H-111 UNIREA (Unity). Victor Tinerean, private publisher. Youngstown, Ohio. 1915-16. Weekly. In Romanian.

Religious--Romanian Catholic; polemics against GLASUL VREMII (retrospective).

H-112 URZICA (The Nettle). Patrichie Todoran; later Nicolae Boer, Sr., private publishers. Wirton, W. Va.; later Martinsferry, Ohio. 1915-18. Monthly. In Romanian.

Humorous.

H-113 VAGABONDUL (The Tramp). Ilarie Pintea and George Sava. Erie, Pa. 1922-25. Irregular. In Romanian.

Humorous.

H-114 VERS (Poem). Nicolae Novac, poet and private publisher. Albany, N.Y. 1951-57. Quarterly. In Romanian.

Literary digest of poetry by a group of Romanian refugees.

H-115 VESTITORUL (The Herald). St. John the Baptist Catholic Church. Detroit, Mich. 1948-49. Monthly. In Romanian.

Parish news.

H-116 VIATA DE DETROIT (Detroit Life). Rev. Fr. Moise Balea. Detroit, Mich. 1941. Irregular. In Romanian.

Local news. The publication had only a brief existence.

H-117 VIATA NOUA (New Life). Gh. Zamfir, Ion J. Banateanu, Rev. Fr. Stefan Opreanu, private publishers. Detroit, Mich. 1933-38. Weekly. In Romanian.

General, local, and cultural news.

H-118 VOCEA POPORULUI (The People's Voice). N. Benchea, private publishers. Indiana Harbor, Ind. 1923. Irregular. In Romanian.

Parish disputes--opposed to Fr. Simion Milhaltian.

H-119 VOCEA POPORULUI (The People's Voice). Detroit, Mich. 1949-50. Irregular. In Romanian.

Political; U.L.R.S.A. internecine fights; opposed to the faction led by N. Balindu.

RETROSPECTIVE ROMANIAN-CANADIAN PERIODICALS

H-120 CANADA. Rev. Valeriu, private publisher. Fort City, Ontario. 1924. Irregular. In Romanian.

Romanian Orthodox education. The publication had only a brief existence.

H-121 DESTEAPTA-TE ROMANE (Awake Thee, Romanian). Constantin Bunescu, private publisher. Hamilton, Ontario. 1915-16. Monthly. In Romanian.

Cultural news.

H-122 ROMANUL CANADIAN (The Canadian Romanian). Aurel Bunescu, private publisher. Hamilton, Ontario. 1917. Irregular. In Romania.

General and local news. The publication had only a brief existence.

I. ROMANIAN-AMERICAN AND CANADIAN PUBLISHING HOUSES, CENTERS OF HOLDINGS, HERITAGE COLLECTIONS, COURSES, AND COMMUNITIES

This section includes seven publishing houses, thirteen centers of holdings and documentation, nine heritage collections and museums, fifteen universities offering courses in Romanian language or on Romanian civilization and culture, as well as ninety-eight Romanian communities in America and Canada.

All items within each subdivision are arranged alphabetically and annotated.

Publishing houses are listed only if they regularly publish books, pamphlets, and other materials in addition to or without newspapers or other periodicals. Houses that issue only newspapers and other periodicals are included in part 2, section H of this guide.

Centers of holdings are included only if they have extensive and specialized collections on the subject, or if they have deposits of important manuscripts and other valuable materials. The list of Romanian heritage collections and museums is compiled in the same spirit.

ROMANIAN-AMERICAN AND CANADIAN PUBLISHING HOUSES

America

I-1   AMERICAN ROMANIAN ACADEMY OF ARTS AND SCIENCES. 265 Lee Street, Oakland, Calif. 04610.

   Books on Romanian culture: language, literature, history.

I-2   ASSOCIATION OF ROMANIAN CATHOLICS OF AMERICA. 4309 Olcott Avenue; East Chicago, Ind. 46312.

   Religious literature, ethnic publications of interest to youth.

I-3   ROMANIAN BAPTIST ASSOCIATION OF THE UNITED STATES. c/o

Rev. Danila Pascu, 9410 Clifton Boulevard, Cleveland, Ohio 44102.

Religious literature of interest to members and churches.

I-4 ROMANIAN ORTHODOX EPISCOPATE OF AMERICA--PUBLISHING
DEPARTMENT. 11341 Woodward Avenue, Detroit, Mich. 48202.

Religious literature, books for children and youth on Romanian
ethnic values, cooking, sports, songs, as well as other subjects
of interest to parishes and their members.

I-5 ROMANIAN ORTHODOX MISSIONARY ARCHDIOCESE IN AMERICA--
PUBLISHING DEPARTMENT. 19959 Riopelle Street, Detroit, Mich.
48203.

Religious literature, pamphlets regarding the history of the Romanian Orthodox Church in Canada and America and its ties
with the land of origin.

I-6 UNION AND LEAGUE OF ROMANIAN SOCIETIES OF AMERICA.
720 Williamson Building, 215 Euclid Avenue, Cleveland, Ohio 44114.

Books and pamphlets on the history of the organization, anni-
versary albums with pictures, literature for youth, poetry, as
well as phonodiscs.

Canada

I-7 ROMANIAN CANADIAN PUBLISHING COMPANY. 1862 Eglinton
Avenue, West, Toronto, Ontario.

Miscellaneous literature.

CENTERS OF HOLDINGS AND DOCUMENTATION IN AMERICA

I-8 ASSOCIATION OF ROMANIAN CATHOLICS OF AMERICA. 4309
Olcott Avenue, East Chicago, Ind. 46312.

Official records of the organization (announcements, convoca-
tions, reports, minutes of meetings) since it came into existence; UNIREA periodicals; several hundred books on Romania,
its history and culture, and on the Romanian Catholics (Eastern Rite) in America and Romania.

I-9 THE CHURCH OF JESUS CHRIST OF LATTER DAY SAINTS. 50 East
North Temple, Salt Lake City, Utah 84150.

The Genealogical Society of this church has an outstanding

library and documentation center collecting genealogy data from all around the world. So far, its holdings exceed 130,000 books and 800,000 rolls of films. The Romanian section comprises more than 500 books and films dealing with Romanian history, maps, emigration, populations of various regions, and vital records (birth, marriage, death) from Bistrita-Nassaud, Iasi, Suceava, Caras-Severin, Constanta, Timisoara, Transylvania, going back to the eighteenth century.

I-10 CLEVELAND ROMANIAN CULTURAL AND ART CENTER. (Annex of the St. Mary's Romanian Orthodox Church). 3256 Warren Road, Cleveland, Ohio 44111.

Library of more than two thousand books in English and Romanian on Romania and about Romanian Americans; largest Romanian American and Canadian ethnographic museum, including peasant costumes, embroideries, weaving, wood carvings, rugs, icons, coats of arms; large collection of paintings by noted Romanian and Romanian American artists; sculptures, furniture.

I-11 IMMIGRATION HISTORY RESEARCH CENTER--ROMANIAN AMERICAN COLLECTION. University of Minnesota. 826 Berry Street. St. Paul, Minn. 55114.

About two hundred monographs on Romanian Americans, their history, churches of all three denominations (Baptist, Catholic, and Eastern Orthodox), calendars issued by these churches, the Union and League of Romanian Societies of America, twenty-two serial titles, and three manuscript collections donated by the Iuliu Maniu American Romanian Relief Foundation (archival material covering 1953-65), the Romanian Orthodox Episcopate of America (archival material covering 1906-75), and The Union and League of Romanian Societies of America (archival material covering 1900-1958).

I-12 IULIU MANIU AMERICAN ROMANIAN RELIEF FOUNDATION. 55 West Forty-second Street, New York, N.Y. 10036.

Library of about five hundred books, pamphlets, and periodicals regarding Romania, its culture and history, as well as Romanian Americans; archival material (minutes, letters, reports) since 1965; collection of Romanian folk art--costumes, embroidery, paintings, wood carvings.

I-13 NEW YORK PUBLIC RESEARCH LIBRARY. Fifth Avenue and Forty-second Street, New York, N.Y. 10036.

Romanian American history; some Romanian American periodicals, extensive collection (2000 books) on Romanian history, fiction, statistics, economy, scientific publications, and encyclopedias.

I-14   PITTSBURGH UNIVERSITY LIBRARIES. 261 Hillmann Library, Pittsburgh, Pa. 15260.

Collection of about six hundred books on Romanian history, literature, folklore, costumes, ethnography; Romanian Americans; a special Romanian Room (furniture, paintings, architecture) in the Cathedral of Learning.

I-15   ROMANIAN LIBRARY. 200 East Thirty-eighth Street, New York, N.Y. 10036.

An agency of the Romanian government, with holdings on Romania; some materials are on Romanian Americans and Canadians; might be instrumental in getting materials from the Library of the Romanian Academy of Sciences, which has a sizable collection of books and periodicals on Romanian Americans.

I-16   ROMANIAN ORTHODOX EPISCOPATE OF AMERICA. 2522 Grey Tower Road, Jackson, Mich. 49201.

Archival material (minutes, reports, communications, letters), library on Romania, its culture, history, religion, as well as on Romanian Americans; sponsors the development of the Romanian American Heritage Center for study and research purposes. Donated the largest part of its archival holdings to the Immigration History Research Center, University of Minnesota.

I-17   SYRACUSE UNIVERSITY LIBRARY. Syracuse, N.Y. 13210.

Depository place for Peter Neagoe's papers consisting of manuscripts, letters, working notes, and so forth. Of interest to researchers and scholars.

I-18   UNION AND LEAGUE OF ROMANIAN SOCIETIES OF AMERICA. 720 Williamson Building, 215 Euclid Avenue, Cleveland, Ohio 44114.

Archival material of the organization since 1959; materials covering the period of 1900-1958 were donated to the Immigration History Research Center, University of Minnesota; collection of books, pamphlets, and periodicals issued by the Union and Leage, as well as other Romanian American and Canadian organizations; audiovisual materials.

CENTERS OF HOLDINGS AND DOCUMENTATION IN CANADA

I-19   HAMILTON MULTICULTURAL CENTRE. 35 Catharine Street, South, Hamilton, Ontario.

Research materials (books and pamphlets) on various ethnic groups living in Hamilton. Covers their contribution to

Canada. The Romanian section comprises more than one hundred books and brochures dealing with Romania, its history, culture, and other aspects. Some materials are on Romanian Canadians or Americans.

I-20   TORONTO PUBLIC LIBRARY. 40 Orchard View Boulevard, Toronto, Ontario.

A collection of Romanian and English books, mostly on Romanian history, civilization, and culture. Also, Romanian literature and customs. Few materials on Romanian Canadians. Organizes exhibits devoted to Romanian heritage.

ROMANIAN HERITAGE COLLECTIONS AND MUSEUMS

Illinois

I-21   THE ART INSTITUTE OF CHICAGO. South Michigan Avenue, Chicago, III. 60603.

Valuable collection of works--bronze, marble and drawings-- by Constantin Brancusi, sculptor.

New York

I-22   THE BROOKLYN MUSEUM. Eastern Parkway and Washington Avenue, Brooklyn, N.Y. 11238.

A sizable collection of Romanian national costumes from various regions.

I-23   THE IULIU MANIU FOUNDATION. 55 West Forty-second Street. New York, N.Y. 10036.

A valuable collection of Romanian national costumes, paintings, wood work, embroidery, and rugs.

I-24   THE METROPOLITAN MUSEUM OF ART. Fifth Avenue and Eightieth Street, New York, N.Y. 10028.

A collection of Romanian National costumes, armory, and some paintings.

I-25   THE MUSEUM OF MODERN ART. 11 West Fifty-third Street, New York, N.Y. 10019.

A sizable collection of works--marble and bronze--by Constantin Brancusi, sculptor.

I-26   THE SOLOMON R. GUGGENHEIM MUSEUM. Fifth Avenue and
Eighty-ninth Street, New York, N.Y. 10028.

>   An important collection of works--marble, oak wood, chestnut
>   wood, and so forth--by Constantin Brancusi, sculptor.

Ohio

I-27   CLEVELAND ROMANIAN CULTURAL & ART CENTER.   3256 Warren
Road, Cleveland, Ohio 44111.

>   The best and most comprehensive Romanian heritage collection
>   in America or Canada. Consists of Romanian folk art, sculp-
>   ture, paintings, peasant costumes, rugs, icons, coats of arms.

Pennsylvania

I-28   PHILADELPHIA MUSEUM OF ART.   Benjamin Franklin Parkway/Spring
Garden Street, Philadelphia, Pa. 19101.

>   Sizable collection of works--marble, bronze, onyx, and wood
>   --by Constantin Brancusi, sculptor.

I-29   ROMANIAN CLASSROOM, PITTSBURGH UNIVERSITY.   Cathedral of
Learning, Pittsburgh, Pa. 15260.

>   Sculpture, interior decoration, paintings, furniture.

ROMANIAN LANGUAGE AND CULTURE COURSES IN AMERICAN UNIVERSITIES

I-30   COLUMBIA UNIVERSITY. New York, N.Y. 10027.

>   Romanian language and civilization courses for undergraduate
>   and graduate students.

I-31   CORNELL UNIVERSITY. Ithaca, N.Y. 14853.

>   Romanian language courses.

I-32   EAST TEXAS STATE UNIVERSITY. Commerce, Tex. 75428.

>   Romanian culture and history on a comparative basis with
>   other cultures.

I-33   GEORGIA, UNIVERSITY OF. Athens, Ga. 30602.

>   Romanian language course.

I-34 KENT STATE UNIVERSITY. Kent, Ohio. 44242.
Romanian language, culture, and civilization for undergraduate and graduate students.

I-35 KENTUCKY, UNIVERSITY OF. Lexington, Ky. 40506.
Romanian language course.

I-36 MICHIGAN, UNIVERSITY OF. Ann Arbor, Mich. 48109.
Romanian language courses.

I-37 NORTH CAROLINA, UNIVERSITY OF. Chapel Hill, N.C. 27514.
Romanian language, literature, and folklore courses.

I-38 OHIO STATE UNIVERSITY. Columbus, Ohio 43210.
Romanian language, culture, and civilization courses.

I-39 PITTSBURGH, UNIVERSITY OF. Pittsburgh, Pa. 15260.
Course on Constantin Brancusi's sculpture.

I-40 PORTLAND STATE UNIVERSITY. Portland, Oreg. 97207.
Romanian language and literature.

I-41 ROCHESTER, UNIVERSITY OF. Rochester, N.Y. 14627.
Romanian language, culture, and civilization courses.

I-42 SOUTH FLORIDA, UNIVERSITY OF. Tampa, Fl. 33620.
Romanian language course.

I-43 U.S. INTERNATIONAL UNIVERSITY. San Diego, Calif. 92101.
Romanian culture compared to other cultures.

I-44 WASHINGTON, UNIVERSITY OF. Seattle, Wash. 98195.
Romanian language courses.

I-44a YALE UNIVERSITY. New Haven, Conn. 06520.
Romanian language course.

NOTE: Courses are subject to yearly changes.

ROMANIAN-AMERICAN AND CANADIAN COMMUNITIES

America

I-45   Arizona
      Phoenix

I-46   California
      La Canada
      Los Angeles
      Oakland
      San Francisco

I-47   Connecticut
      Bridgeport

I-48   District of Columbia
      Washington

I-49   Florida
      Hollywood

I-50   Illinois
      Aurora
      Chicago
      Lansing

I-51   Indiana
      East Chicago
      Fort Wayne
      Garret
      Gary
      Hobbart
      Indianapolis
      Merrilville
      Terre Haute

I-52   Massachusetts
      Southbridge
      Worcester

I-53   Michigan
      Berkley
      Dearborn
      Detroit
      Grass Lake
      Highland Park
      Pontiac
      Southfield
      Warren

I-54   Minnesota
      St. Paul
      South St. Paul

I-55   Missouri
      St. Joseph
      St. Louis

I-56   Nebraska
      Bellevue
      Omaha

I-57   New Jersey
      Bordentown
      Roebling
      Trenton

I-58   New York
      Buffalo
      New York City

I-59   Ohio
      Akron
      Alliance
      Cambridge
      Canton
      Chesterfield

Cincinnati
Hubbard
Lorain
Niles
Salem
Toledo
Warren
Youngstown

Erie
Farrell
McKeesport
New Castle
Philadelphia
Sharon
West Homestead

I-61   Rhode Island

Woonsocket

I-60   Pennsylvania

Aliquippa
Allentown
Beaver Falls
Bethlehem
Ellwood

I-62   West Virginia

Weirton

Canada

I-63   Alberta

Boian
Calgary
Edmonton
Hairy Hill
Hamlin
Malin
Manning
Peace River

Kitchener
Timmins
Toronto
Windsor

I-67   Quebec

Lachine
Montreal

I-64   British Columbia

Vancouver

I-68   Saskatchewan

Assinboia
Canora
Dysart
Elm Spring
Flintoff
Kayville
Mac Nutt
Marcelin
Pierceland
Regina
Wood Mountain

I-65   Manitoba

Lennard
Shell Valley
Winnipeg

I-55   Ontario

Hamilton

J. CULTURAL MISCELLANEOUS

CONSTANTIN BRANCUSI IN AMERICAN MUSEUMS

J-1   THE ART INSTITUTE OF CHICAGO

      Ancient Figure, limestone, 1909
      Sleeping Muse, bronze, 1910
      Two Penguins, white marble, 1914
      Three Infants, pen and India ink, no date
      Head of a Woman, pen and red brown ink, no date

J-2   THE MUSEUM OF FINE ARTS, HOUSTON, TEXAS

      Muse, polished brass, 1914

J-3   MUSEUM OF MODERN ART, NEW YORK

      Maistra, white marble, 1912
      Miss Pogany, bronze, 1913
      The New Born, polished bronze, 1915
      Birth in Space, polished bronze, 1919
      The Fish, gray marble, 1930

J-4   PHILADELPHIA MUSEUM OF ART

      Maiastra, white marble, 1912
      Miss Pogany, white marble, 1913
      The Prodigal Son, oak, 1914
      The New Born, marble, 1915
      Arch, old oak, 1917
      Chimera, oak, 1918
      The Princess, polished bronze, 1918
      Bench, old oak, 1918
      Torso of a Young Girl, onyx, 1922
      The White Negress, marble, 1924
      Bird in Space, yellow marble, 1925
      Bird in Space, polished bronze, 1925
      Miss Pogany, marble, 1931

J-5   SOLOMON R. GUGGENHEIM MUSEUM, NEW YORK

Portrait of George, marble, 1911
The First Step, oak, 1920
Adam and Eve, chestnut and old oak, 1921
Socrates, wood, 1923
The King of Kings, wood, 1937
Flying Turtle, marble, 1941
Nude, pencil on board, no date
Birds on Sky, no date

J-6   UNIVERSITY OF NEBRASKA

The Princess, marble, 1916
Head of a Young Girl, pencil, no date

NOTE: The date mentioned after each work is the year of its completion.

GEORGE ENESCO'S COMPOSITIONS

J-7   Main compositions arranged chronologically:

Romanian Poem, 1897
Pastoral Phantasy, 1898
Octet for String Instruments, 1900
Romanian Rhapsody No. 1 in A Major, 1901
Symphony Concerto for Piano and Orchestra, 1901
Romanian Rhapsody No. 2 in D Major, 1902
Suite No. 1 in Classic Style, 1903
Symphony No. 1, 1905
Dixtuor for Wind Instruments, 1906
Quartet for Piano, 1909-11
Symphony No. 2, 1913
Suite No. 2 in C Major, 1915
Symphony No. 3, 1919-20
Quartet for String Instruments, 1921
Suite No. 3 in Rustic Style, 1938
Suite "Impressions from Childhood," 1940
Quartet for Piano, 1944
Quartet for String Instruments, 1952
Symphony for 12 Soloist Instruments, 1954

NOTE: The date after each work indicates the year it was written.

JEAN NEGULESCO'S AMERICAN MOVIES

J-8   The movies directed by Negulesco are arranged chronologically:

Singapore Woman, 1941
The Conspirators, 1944

The Mask of Demetrios, 1944
Humoresque, 1946
Nobody Lives Forever, 1946
Three Strangers, 1946
Deep Valley, 1947
Johnny Belinda, 1948
Road House, 1948
The Forbidden Street, 1949
The Mudlark, 1950
Under My Skin, 1950
Three Came Home, 1950
Take Care of My Little Girl, 1951
Lure of the Wilderness, 1952
Lydia Bailey, 1952
Phone Call from a Stranger, 1952
Titanic, 1953
How to Marry a Millionaire, 1953
Three Coins in the Fountain, 1954
Woman's World, 1954
Daddy Long Legs, 1955
Rains of Ranchipur, 1955
Boy on a Dolphin, 1957
A Certain Smile, 1958
The Gift of Love, 1958
Best of Everything, 1959
Count Your Blessings, 1959
Jessica, 1962
The Pleasure Seekers, 1964

J-9   Movies authored by Negulesco arranged chronologically:

Fight for Your Lady, 1937
Beloved Brat, 1938
Swiss Miss, 1938
Rio, 1939

GEORGE ZOLNAY'S WORKS IN AMERICA

J-10	California	U.S. Customs House monument. San Francisco
J-11	Georgia	Gen. Bartow monument, Savannah Gen. McLaws monument, Savannah
J-12	Kentucky	Soldiers' monument, Owensboro
J-13	Massachusetts	Labor monument, New Bedford
J-14	Missouri	Confederate monument, St. Louis Pierre Laclede monument, St. Louis

J-15	Tennessee	Sam Davis monument, Nashville
		Soldiers monument, Nashville
		War Memorial and Parthenon, Nashville

J-16	Virginia	Edgar Allan Poe statue, University of Virginia, Charlottesville
		Jefferson Davis monument, Richmond
		Winnie Davis monument, Richmond

J-17	Washington, D.C.	Sequoyah statue, U.S. Capitol, Washington, D.C.

INDEXES

NAME INDEX

This index includes all authors, editors, compilers, translators, and other contributors to annotated works. It also lists names of several noted personalities encountered in some annotations. Numbers refer to entry numbers and alphabetization is letter by letter.

A

Abramovici, Miron H-17
Abramson, M. C-75
Adamic, Louis A-36
Alexander the Good F-108
Alexandru Cel Bun F-108
Alexe, Gheorghe H-7
Alroy, G.C. C-75
American Council for Nationalities
    Service A-27, B-159
American Institute of Writing Research
    A-39
Anagnostache, Gheorghe C-14
Anagnostache, Mary B-143
Anderson, James M. A-21
Andreescu, Stefan D-36
Andrica, Theodore A-36, C-28,
    C-32, C-33, C-34, H-75, H-113
Andronescu, Serban A-39, B-160
Angelescu, Dr. F-119
Antonovici, Constantin B-112, B-140
Asad-Weis, M. B-45
Ash, Lee A-13
Association of Romanian Catholics of
    America B-9
Augustus, Emperor B-54
Axelrad, Philip B-106, H-102

B

Balas, Edith B-119
Balasu, Gheorghe H-24
Balea, Fr. Moise B-19, H-116
Balindu, N. H-119
Banateanu, Ion (John) J. H-71,
    H-117
Barbu, I.N. H-69
Barbu, Dr. Valer E-11, E-12
Barbu, Zevedei C-73
Barbul, Gheorghe D-2
Barbulescu, Constantin E-16
Barlea, Octavian D-30
Barnes, Sherman B-38
Barnutiu, Simion F-101
Barsan, Vasile C. C-62, D-37
Barton, Joseph J. C-29
Basarab, Vasile H-35, H-105
Belknap, Gen. William D-4, D-5
Benchea, N. H-118
Bercovici, Konrad B-45, C-26,
    C-30
Bocioaga, Fr. Alexandru H-34
Boer, Nicolae H-112
Bogart, Gary L. A-10
Bogdan, John G-44
Bohar, N.C. C-22

Name Index

Boian, F.A. H–61
Boian, George F. H–15
Borza, John, Jr. D–6
Botez, Ion A–40
Bothezat, George De E–10
Brancoveanu, Constantin F–77
Brancusi, Constantin I–25, I–26,
  I–28, J–1, J–2, J–3, J–4, J–5,
  J–6
Bratu, Petre B–22
Brauer, Gerald B–35
Brown, Francis C–4, C–5, C–6
Brummer Gallery B–121
Bucur, Nicholas C–48
Budai, Ioan H–92
Bunescu, Constantin H–121, H–122
Butiu, Constantin D–28
Buttlar, Lois A–15

C

Callimachi, Princess Anne-Marie
  B–51
Carja, Ion B–60, B–61
Carnician, Andrei G–63
Carol I, King F–70
Carol II, King F–90, H–64
Carpenter, Niles C–89
Carson, Jack B–156
Cassou, Jean B–117
Champion, Selwyn G. B–40
Chanin, A.L. B–124
Cioran, E[mil]. M. B–1, B–2
Ciukurescu, George G–44
Cloanta, Olimpiu H–29
Coatu, Ovid G–30
Cohen, J.M. B–31
Cook, Dorothy B–45, B–141, B–142
Corbett, Scott B–95, B–96
Craciunas, Silviu B–62
Cretzianu, Alexandre C–74
Crisan, George B–6
Cristo-Loveanu, Elie B–103, G–31,
  G–43, G–61
Cuza, Alexandru Ion F–53

D

Daniel-Rops, B–54
Daschevici, Eglantina B–79

Davidoff, Henry B–41
Denny, Norman B–52
Disescu, D. H–81
Donev, George B–162
Donovan, Maria K. E–24
Dragos, N. H–69
Drugociu, Ion H–52
Drugociu, Nicolae H–110
Drutzu, Serban C–7, C–8
Dudley, D. B–126
Dudley, Guilford B–37
Duma, Solomon H–78
Dumitriu, Petru B–50, B–51, B–52
Dunca, Captain Nicholas F–19
Dunham, Donald C–49
Dvoichenko-Markov, Demetrius D–3
Dwyer, Joseph D. A–17

E

Eastman, Mary Huse B–84
Eliade, Mircea B–28, B–29, B–30,
  B–31, B–32, B–33, B–34, B–35,
  B–53, B–63
Elizabeth, Queen B–84, F–115
Eminescu, Mihail F–81
Enesco, George B–163, B–164,
  J–7
Epstein, L. B–46
Ewen, David B–172

F

Faget, J.T. H–16
Fekett, Sofron S. D–23
Ferdinand I, King F–125, F–126
Fidell, Estelle A–10, A–12, B–46
Fillman, George D–8, D–9, D–11
Fischer-Galati, Stephen A–6
Florea, John A–38
Florescu, Radu D–34, D–35
Fogarassy, O. B–104
Forsberg, Fr. Mark F–50
Foster, Joanna B–94
Foy, Felician B–3
Franklin, Benjamin D–3
Fremont, General John D–8

G

Galitzi, Christine Avghi C–9, C–15

Name Index

McKimmey, J. B–46
McNally, Raymond T. D–34, D–35
Mamford, L. B–128
Maniu, Iuliu F–63, H–83
Marcu, Lucian H–55
Mark, Linda A–4
Marquis Who's Who B–27, E–2, E–8, E–20
Marutescu, Constantin G–64
Mary, Queen B–84
Mead, Frank S. B–5
Michael, King F–88, F–94
Michael the Brave F–76
Mihail, Petre H–11
Mihai Viteazul. See Michael the Brave
Mihaltean, Nicholas C–57
Mihaltian, Fr. Simion H–118
Milburn, F. B–170
Miller, Wayne Charles C–1, C–2
Miroiu, Mihai B–107, B–108
Moldovan, Andrei H–58
Monro, Isabel S. B–45, B–141
Monro, Kate B–142
Morand, Paul B–121
Moraru, Glicherie H–101, H–109
Morgan, Jean A–26
Moritz, Charles B–42, B–150, E–3
Motok, Eugenia C. C–31
Motzu, Joan A–42
Muresan, Andrei F–26
Muresan, Rev. George B–11, D–27, D–30
Muresan, Rev. Octavian H–107
Musi, Vasile H–33

N

Nan, George A–24
Nandris, Grigore B–105
Nasso, Christine B–85
Neagoe, Peter B–45, B–47, B–48, B–55, B–56, B–57, B–66, B–76, I–17
Neamtu–Martin, H–101, H–109
Negoesco, Steve C–69
Negulescu, Jean B–154, B–155, J–8
Negulescu, Paul H–94
Newman, Charles B–1
Nicholas, Prince F–125

Nimigeanu, Dimitru B–67
Novac, Nicolae B–77, B–80, H–114

O

Obreanu, P.E. E–9
O'Brien, J. B–48
Ocneanu, Traian B–181, C–56
Olesky, Walter E–27
Opreanu, Fr. Stefan H–93, H–117
Ovid, (poet) B–54

P

Pach, W. B–131
Palade, Dr. George Emil E–1, E–2, E–3, E–4, E–5, E–6, E–7
Panciuk, Rev. Fr. Mircea B–23
Papana, Alex E–17, E–18
Partington, Paul B–148
Parvu, Ilie I. D–13
Pascu, C.R. C–35
Pascu, Liviu H–106
Pearce, Catherine O. B–99
Pearson, Kenneth A–24
Pei, Mario B–103
Petit, Alexandre D–32
Petra, Nicolae B–82
Petrino, George H–70
Pintea, George H–92
Pintea, Ilarie H–113
Podea, Fr. Ion C–11, H–66, H–97
Polvay, Marina E–29
Pomutz, Gen. George D–4, D–6, F–20
Popa, Eli B–78
Popa-Deleu, Aurelia C–58, C–59
Popa-Deleu, John A–41
Popescu, Aureliu C–36
Popovici, Andrei C–8, C–16, C–17, C–37
Popovici, Rev. Ioan H–68
Popp, Fr. Nathaniel B–11, G–30
Porea, Cornelia C–60
Posteuca, Vasile B–75, B–81, B–82
Pound, Ezra B–76, B–121

Q

Quinn, John B-121

R

Rapaport, Samuel E-23
Ravage, M.E. B-68
Ravage-Tresfort, Louise B-68
Reich, Hary H-80
Rex, Frederick C-20
Ricketts, Mac L. B-53
Roberts, Peter C-44
Roman, Iancu H-38, H-47
Roman, Stella B-177
Romanian Orthodox Episcopate of America B-13, B-14, B-15
Romanian Orthodox Missionary Archdiocese in America B-26
Romanian Orthodox Missionary Episcopate in America B-24
Romanul, Alexander B-176
Romanul, Michael B-176
Romanul, Myron B-176
Romanul, Victor B-176
Romcea, Charles C-64
Roosevelt, President Franklin Delano F-47
Rosenberg, Sondra B-100
Roucek, Joseph S. C-4, C-5, C-6
Rousseau, Arsene G-34, G-39

S

Saarinen, A.B. B-133
Sabau, Mrs. George G-52, G-65
Saguna, Andrei H-33
Sakall, Dan B-69
Sandburg, Carl B-121
Sandulescu, Jaques B-58, B-70
Sava, George H-113
Schiopul, Iosif C-12, H-66
Seceni, Alexandru G-40, G-43, G-57, G-58
Selisteanul, Illie Martin D-1
Sells, Lytton B-54
Serban, Andrei B-150
Sheehan, Etna B-10
Sherman, Nancy B-102
Shirey, D.L. B-135

Sickels, Alice L. B-151
Sitea, Teodor H-179
Slonimsky, Nicholas B-163
Smarandescu, Nicolae B-179
Soby, J.T. B-136
Solomon, Michael B-71
Solomon R. Guggenheim Museum B-122
Spear, Athena B-120
Stan, Anisoara B-72, E-30
Stanculescu, George C-19
Stanculescu, Gheorghe H-62, H-63, H-77, H-98
Stefan, John C-23
Stefan Cel Mare F-33
Stein, Gertrude B-76
Stephan the Great F-33
Stevenson, Mary Park B-53
Stewart, Jean B-64
Stoica, Vasile C-40, D-31, D-33
Stoicoiu, Virgiliu C-79
Stroescu, Vasile F-133
Sturtevant, Donald F. B-49
Sufana, Ioan H-41
Sun Newspapers and Nationalities Service Center A-22
Sylva, Carmen. See Elizabeth, Queen

T

Taflan, Alexander E-19
Tancock, J. B-137
Tashoff, Sol B-161
Teiuseanu, Major Liviu F-102
Teodorescu, Paul G. D-29
Teodoru, Constantin V. E-20
Teppich, John E-30
Terzis, John G-34, G-47
Theodorescu, E.C. B-59
Theodorescu, Radu E-8
Theodoru, Nina B-83
Theodoru, Stefan G. A-43, B-83
Thernstrom, Stephan A-25
Tifft, Wilton C-45
Tinerean, Victor H-111
Todoran, Patrichie H-112
Toma, Mike G. C-43
Toma, Radu A-5

Name Index

Tomuletz, John B-180

Traianus, Marcus Ulpius. See Trajan, Emperor

Trajan, Emperor F-55, F-63, F-73, F-75, F-78, H-61

Trandaphillou, C. G-59

Trask, Willard R. B-28, B-34

Trifa, Bishop Valerian A-35, B-20, B-21, D-32

Trutza, Peter B-8, C-6, C-21

U

Ungureanu, Gheorghe H-62

U.S. Commissioner of Immigration C-13

U.S. Department of Commerce, Bureau of the Census C-81, C-82, C-83, C-84, C-85, C-86, C-87

U.S. Department of Labor C-88

U.S. Department of War D-5

U.S. Library of Congress A-6

University of Pittsburgh, Achievements of the Nationality Committees B-144

Ure, Jean C-61

Ursul, George R. B-25

V

Valahu, Mugur A-37

Valeriu, Rev. H-120

Vamasescu, Nicolae H-53

Vance, J. B-46

Varciu, Theodore B-162

Vasiliu, John W. E-15

Vasiliu, Mircea B-73, B-74, B-85, B-86, B-87, B-88, B-89, B-90, B-91, B-92, B-93, B-95, B-96, B-97, B-98, B-99, B-100, B-101, B-102

Vernescu, Alexandru H-50, H-96

Vintila, Horia B-54

Vlad, Ana F-46

W

Waldo, Myra E-28

Wasserman, Paul A-26

Watson, Donald B-43

Weirich, Jerry B-149

Wertsman, Vladimir C-3

West, Dorothy H. A-12

Williams, Sam P. A-14

Williams, W.C. B-138

Wilson, Angus B-121

Wilson, Woodrow F-111

Wright, Helen E-23

Wynar, Anna T. A-33

Wynar, Lubomyr R. A-15, A-20, A-32, A-33

Z

Zamfir, Gheorghe H-117

Zamfirescu, Nicolae H-30, H-57

Zolnay, George B-113, J-9, J-10, J-11, J-12, J-13, J-14, J-15, J-16, J-17

TITLE INDEX

This index comprises titles of books, pamphlets, reports, dissertations, articles, and newspapers and other periodicals mentioned in Section H. In some cases, lengthy titles have been shortened. Titles preceded by an asterisk contain information on Romanian-Canadians or were written by Romanian-Canadian authors. Numbers refer to entry numbers, and alphabetization is letter by letter.

A

Aaron Copland B-99
Actiunea Romaneasca H-1
Adevarul H-28, H-29
"Aida Was Her Signature Role" B-177
Album Aniversar B-13
Allright H-30
America: Romanian News H-2
America Literara H-31
American Art Annual B-113
American International Encyclopedia Cookbook E-26
American in the Making: The Life and Story of an Immigrant B-68
"Americanizing the Romanian Language in the United States" B-109
American Men and Women of Science E-1
American Noastra H-32
American Orthodox Youth: A Short History B-16
American Romanian Review H-3
Americans Abroad B-76
*America Si Romanii Din America C-10
Analytical Economics: Issues and Answers C-70

Annual Report of the Commission of Immigration C-88
Antonovici B-140
"ARCAYD, Organization for Romanian Catholic Youth" B-11
Are There Any More at Home Like You? B-100
Are You Considering Psychoanalysis? E-13
Around the World in New York C-26
Around the World in St. Paul B-151
"Art Exhibition at Guggenheim Museum" B-124
"A.T.A. Biography Service-Romania" B-148
"Automatic Control of Aircraft" E-16
Ayer Directory of Publications A-29

B

Back to Newton, a Challenge to Einstein's Theory of Relativity E-10
Baker's Biographical Dictionary of Musicians B-163
Balkan Cooking E-25
Baseball Encyclopedia C-68

Title Index

Title Index

T

Talmaciri din Lirica Amerindiana
B-77
Talmaciu, Pronuntator si Dictionar
Englez-Roman si Roman-Englez
B-106
Talmaciu Roman Englezesc Pentru
Romanii Aflatori Astazi in America
B-104
"Teatrul Romanesc in Coloniile
Noastre" B-153
Tesala H-103
There Is My Heart B-57
They Crossed Mountains B-72
Thirteenth Census of the United
States in the Year 1910 C-82
"Three Nobel Laureats in Medicine"
E-7
Time to Keep B-66
"Tinerii Romani Aflati in Liceele
Americane in 1930" C-67
Transilvania H-104
Traznetul H-105
Tribuna H-106, H-107, H-108,
H-109
Tribuna Romana H-110
Twelfth Census of the United States
in the Year 1900 C-81
Twenty Years of Pictorial Review:
1952-1972 B-15
"Two Romanians in the Civil War"
D-6

U

Ulrich's International Periodical
Directory A-31
Ultimul Invins B-80
"Un Brav Ostean Roman American"
D-15
Unirea H-21, H-111
Unirea Almanac B-9, H-22
"University of Chicago Religion Pro-
fessor Mircea Eliade . . . " B-39
Urzica H-112
"USF Wins One for the U.N." C-69

V

Vagabondul H-113

Vers H-114
Versuri B-83
Vestitorul H-115
*Vestitorul Roman Canadian H-26
Viata de Detroit H-116
Viata In Christos H-23
Viata Noua H-117
"Viata Romaneasca din America"
C-19, C-35
"Vlad the Impaler--Dracula" D-36
Vocea Poprului H-118, H-119
Voluntarii Romani din America
D-13

W

Wallachian Flag A-43
"We Are Proud of Nicholas Daramus,
Jr." D-22
"Wedding in Youngstown" C-60
"What Is ARCA?" B-12
"What Price Romanian Customs?"
C-48
What's Happening? B-91
"What You Should Know about
Compressibility" E-18
Which Way the Melting Pot? B-74
Winning a Wife and other Stories
B-48
Who's Who in America B-27, E-2
E-8
Who's Who in American Art B-112
Who's Who in Romanian America
A-39, B-160
Who's Who in the East E-20
World is Many Things B-92
World Treasury of Proverbs from
Twenty-Five Languages B-41

Y

*Yearbook of American and Canadian
Churches B-4
Year Goes Around B-93

Z

Zalmoxis, the Vanishing God: Comparative Studies in the History of
Religions B-34

SUBJECT INDEX

This index covers main areas of interest from both the Bibliographic Compendium and Directories Addendum. Numbers refer to entry numbers, and alphabetization is letter by letter.

A

Acculturation and assimilation in
    language B-109
    religion C-21
    social and economic life C-9
America, Romanian presence and
    participation in
    Colonial period D-3
    Civil War D-4 to D-10
    Spanish-American War D-11
    World War I D-12 to D-15
    World War II D-16 to D-21
Antonovici, Constantin B-112, B-140
Autobiographies, Romanians in
    America B-60 to B-70, B-72 to
    B-74
    Canada B-71
Aviation E-16 to E-19

B

Balea, Moise B-19
Barbu, Dr. Valer E-11
Barsan, Vasile C. C-62
Biological Sciences E-1 to E-7
Boian, Canada, Romanians in C-43
Brancusi, Constantin B-114 to B-120

C

Canada, Romanians in A-24, C-7,
    C-8, C-41
Canton, Ohio, Romanians in C-32
Carja, Ion B-60, B-61
Centers of holdings and documentation
    on Romanians in
    America I-8 to I-18
    Canada I-19, I-20
Chicago, Romanians in C-20 to
    C-22
Children's literature and illustrations
    biography B-85, B-94
    books B-86 to B-93
    illustrations B-95 to B-102
Churches, directories of
    Romanian Baptist G-1 to G-10
    (America)
    Romanian Catholic G-11 to
    G-28 (America)
    Romanian Orthodox G-29 to
    G-105 (America and Canada)
Cleveland, Ohio, Romanians in
    C-28 to C-31, C-36
Communities, directory of Romanian
    in
    America I-45 to I-62
    Canada I-63 to I-68

Subject Index

Comsa, Dumitru D-15
Cooking, Romanian American and
    Canadian E-24 to E-32
Costumes, Romanian
    articles B-143
    indexes B-141, B-142
Craciunas, Silviu B-62
Customs, popular and religious
    Christmas C-56
    Easter C-57, C-58
    general C-48 to C-55
    wedding C-60

D

Damian, Samuel D-3
Daramus, Nicholas D-22
Detroit, Romanians in A-21
Dracula. See Vlad the Impaler
Dunca, Captain Nicholas D-6 to
    D-8

E

Economics C-70 to C-72
Education C-63, C-65 to C-67
Eliade, Mircea B-27, B-36, B-38,
    B-39, B-63
Embroidery B-146
Enesco, George B-163 to B-170
Engineering E-14, E-15

F

Fairy tales, indexes B-84
Fiction B-50 to B-59
Flags A-43
Florea, John A-38, B-157, B-158
Folk dancing B-183
Folk music, anthologies B-179, B-180,
    B-181
Folk tales C-61
Furniture B-144, B-155

G

Georgescu-Roegen, Nichoalas C-72

H

Hemingway, Ernest B-76

I

Icons B-111
Ileana, Princess E-23
Immigrant life, early C-44 to C-47
Immigration and settlement, Romanians
    in
    America A-21, A-26, C-1 to
      to C-19 (general); C-20 to
      C-40 (regional)
    Canada A-24, C-7, C-8
      (general); C-41 to C-43
      (regional)
Ionesco, Eugene B-42, B-44,
    B-64, B-65

J

Journalism A-36 to A-38

L

Law C-79 to C-81
Leucutia, Dr. Traian E-20 to E-22
Libraries, Romanian Americans in
    A-9
Lorain, Ohio, Romanians in C-33
Lucaciu, Epaminonda B-19

M

Macedo-Romanians C-39, C-40
McKees Rocks, Pennsylvania,
    Romanians in C-38
Mahoning Valley, Ohio, Romanians
    in C-34
Maniu, Iuliu D-26
Mathematics E-8, E-9 (Canada)
Medicine E-20 to E-22. See also
    Psychiatry
Military heroes, Romanian Americans
    D-20, D-21
Movies and television, Romanian
    Americans in B-154 to B-158
Museums, Romanian heritage in
    America I-21 to I-29
Music, Romanians in America
    composers B-163 to B-171
    conductors B-172 to B-174
    performers B-175, B-176

recorded B-182
See also Opera

N

Names, Romanian, meanings of A-42
Neagoe, Peter B-49, B-66
Negulescu, Jean B-154, B-156
New York City, Romanians in C-26, C-27
Nimigeanu, Dumitru B-67
Nursing E-23

O

Opera, Romanians in America B-177, B-178
Organizations and institutions,
Romanians in
America D-23 to D-29 (history);
F-1 to F-76 (directory)
Canada F-77 to F-84 (directory)

P

Painting, Romanians in
America B-111
Canada B-110
Palade, Dr. George Emil E-1 to E-7
Periodicals, Romanians in
America A-27 to A-33 (guide);
H-1 to H-23 (directory)
Canada H-24 to H-27 (directory)
Perlea, Ionel B-171 to B-174
Philadelphia, Romanians in C-37
Philosphy B-1, B-2
Physics E-10
Poetry, Romanian American
anthologies B-78 to B-83
biography B-75 to B-77
Politics C-73 to C-78
Pomutz, General George D-6, D-9, D-10
Posteuca, Vasile B-75
Pound, Ezra B-76
Priests, Romanian in America B-19
Proverbs, anthologies of B-40, B-41
Psychiatry E-11 to E-13
Publishing houses, Romanian in
America I-1 to I-6
Canada I-7

R

Radio programs, Romanian American
B-159 to B-162
Ravage, M.E. B-68
Religion, guides to
general B-3 to B-5
Romanian Baptist B-6 to B-8
Romanian Catholic B-9 to B-12
Romanian Orthodox B-13 to B-26
See also Churches
Religious symbolism B-28 to B-34
Roman, Stella B-177, B-178
Romania, land of origin A-6, C-74, D-30 to D-32
Romanian American Collection A-17
Romanian American Heritage Center A-18
Romanian Americans
bibliographies A-1 to A-9
catalogs A-10 to A-12
library resources A-13 to A-18
Romanian language
conversation books B-104 to B-105
courses directory I-30 to I-44
dictionaries B-106 to B-108
manuals B-103
Romanian Orthodox Episcopate of
America B-17, B-18, B-21
Romanian Orthodox Missionary
Episcopate in America B-24
Romanul, Brothers (Alexander, Michael, Miron, Victor)
B-176
Romcea, Prof. Charles C-64

S

St. Louis, Montana, Romanians in
C-24, C-25
St. Paul, Minnesota, Romanians in
C-23
Sakall, Dan B-69
Sandulescu, Jaques B-70
Sculpture, Romanians in America
articles B-123 to B-139
biographies B-112 to B-115
exhibits B-121, B-122
studies B-115 to B-120